Craig Hughes' new boo[illegible] is FANTASTIC! If you hap[illegible] millions of people who own a small business and feel trapped by the constant work, pressures, and cash challenges, then this book is for you. Through Craig's personal and compelling journey that comes straight from the heart of a humble servant who's "been there - done that," he will guide through the pitfalls to avoid as you move your business from struggle to sustainability and growth. The book will also help prepare you for the inevitable disruptions that will impact your business at some point. No matter what type of business you own, this book will help you improve yourself as a leader, get your business and life back into control and balance, and put you on the path to achieve your dreams.

Brett Blair, High Performance Coach
Author of *From Autopilot to Authentic*

For the past several years, I've been reading over 300 non-fiction books a year. It's been my experience that 85 percent of the books are not worth reading. About 14 percent are pretty good, so only 1 percent of them are worth my time. *The Self-Driving Company* is an absolute 1 percent book. One of the reasons is that Craig has been there, done it, and created a magnificently successful business. There is no substitute for first-hand experience. I highly recommend you read this book.

Dr. Tom Hill
Coauthor of *Chicken Soup for the Entrepreneur's Soul*
Author of *Living at the Summit*

Craig Hughes has a way of taking complex subject matter and boiling it down to its simplest essence. *The Self-Driving Company* is a must-read for any entrepreneur. Cloaked in these pages are pearls of wisdom not found in formulized business theory. His captivating stories, coupled with the lessons learned along the way, paint a pathway for the reader to achieve phenomenal business success.

Doug Damon
CEO, Damon Industries

The Self-Driving Company is a must-read for entrepreneurs who feel trapped by their day-to-day business operations and long for the freedom that being self-employed promises. If you're tired of wearing all the hats, making all the decisions, and doing all the dirty work, then follow the advice of Craig Hughes and get out of the way, so your business can thrive!

John Ruhlin, Founder & CEO of Ruhlin Group
Author of *Giftology*

Craig brilliantly captures the paradoxical nature of owning and running a business in *The Self-Driving Company*. He clearly illustrates how—when building a business—every decision and every choice seems to be counter-intuitive, such as gaining more control by letting go; growing faster by slowing down; and hiring people who are smarter than you to take over your own job. Craig presents a beautiful story of how he created a fast-growing company where people enjoy their work, and he provides a framework that any CEO or manager can apply to their own business.

Jim Canfield
Author of the updated and revised *CEO Tools*

The Self-Driving Company

How Getting Out of the Way Enabled My Business to Thrive

Craig C. Hughes

Stonebrook Publishing
Saint Louis, Missouri

A STONEBROOK PUBLISHING BOOK

Edited by Nancy Erickson, The Book Professor

TheBookProfessor.com

Book cover and interior design by JETLAUNCH.net

Library of Congress Control Number: 2017946091

ISBN: 978-0-9975210-2-3

www.stonebrookpublishing.net

PRINTED IN THE UNITED STATES OF AMERICA

10 9 8 7 6 5 4 3 2 1

I dedicate this book to the love of my life and my best friend, Chris. She has supported my career and our life together every step of the way, and without her I would have nothing.

I also want to acknowledge our children and grandchildren.

Special thanks to my mentor and friend, Dr. Tom Hill; my CEO and friend, Mike Pinckard; and all of our employees and leaders, who create so much value through their perseverance and hard work.

Dad, I forever miss you.

Contents

"Here's where we're going," I told my management team. "In the next five years, our company is going to be the solution, not just locally, but on a national basis."

After the meeting, Mike pulled me aside and asked, "Are you sure that's the direction you want to go? You have a pretty nice lifestyle and profitable company now."

"Yes," I replied. "I really believe in our mission and our team's ability to get things done. I want to push toward this vision."

Again Mike pressed me. "Are you sure? You get to go home every night and be with your family. Going this direction will require a lot of travel to oversee that many locations."

"Mike, I know the travel has to be done, but I'm not the one who's going to do it."

I had now accepted my role as the owner, not a manager, and it gave me the freedom to dream big.

Mike went to work to make the vision a reality.

Introduction

Are you trapped in your own business? Did you think that if you owned a business, you'd enjoy freedom, but the hours and demands of the job tie you down and the financial hazards paralyze you? I've experienced that lack of freedom and the financial paralysis—especially when I first got started. But with the help of my team, I was able to work through the challenges and overcome obstacles when they blocked our way.

And through it all, I learned valuable lessons that I want to share with others who are going through what I went through. So whether you've considered purchasing your own business, are trapped in one now, or don't want to be trapped again, then this book is for you. In these pages, I'll outline my experiences and explain the discoveries made in the thirty-plus years it took for us to transition our company from a very small, inefficient, low-income operation to the point when we were able to unleash our company's potential to create the success we now enjoy. This includes our newest venture, a high-tech startup that has the potential to exceed $1 billion in annual sales in the near future.

You'll bear witness to my transformation from being a slave to my business to making my business work for our team, of which I was just one member. You'll notice how I go from using words like *I* and *mine* to *us* and *ours*, as the business changed from being less about *my* decisions to being about the decisions and direction made by *our* talented team. And you'll read about how we learned to get the best people on board and how to keep them motivated (hint: it's not all about the money).

We'll also examine how we made the transformation from a newbie business, when I didn't have a clue how to run a business and had no knowledge about our industry, to a well-run, well-oiled machine. We created an organization that takes on any challenge, embraces change and disruption, and blazes new trails.

We'll also explore whether owning a business is the best thing for your situation and personality, or if you'd be better off working for someone else who has the necessary appetite for risk that business owners need.

This is my story, but I think you'll be able to transpose my situations to your own experience and, hopefully, develop a corrective plan and a path for a successful future. No matter what business you're in, you can turn your situation around and make your company as relevant as you want it to be.

I'll take you through the early struggles and all the obstacles we faced, to our incredible success today and the opportunities we have for tomorrow. You can use some of the same techniques and the same mindset to unstick your business, no matter what size it is or what industry you're in.

In short, the book you hold in your hand is designed to transform your way of thinking to allow you to achieve your dreams.

1

What Qualifies Me to Own My Own Business?

What does it take to buy a business? Not much. What does it take to run a successful business? Now, that's a different question. Short answer: a tremendous amount of grit and energy and humility. But most of all, it takes a great team. Here's the short version of my journey to business ownership.

Imagine a Monday night, fried chicken night at the Hughes household. My mom would serve a large platter of chicken, enough for my parents, my four sisters, my brother, and me. As soon as the platter hit the table, my hand shot out. I'd stick my fork into the largest chicken breast on the platter and plop it on my plate. Dad would start the blessing, so we'd all settle down and join in.

As soon as the prayer was over, Dad would ask, "Craig, can you please pass me the second-best piece of chicken?"

I was the immature, impulsive child, and Dad was a conservative businessman with a dry sense of humor. A large man, he was a gentle giant and the inspiration for me to become a business owner.

My father commanded a lot of respect in our small delta town in Northeast Arkansas. I thought he was respected because he was the boss and a business owner, but I came to find out that he was respected because of who he was. He was a civic leader and a tireless volunteer. So much so, that he was eventually recognized as Volunteer of the Year for the entire state of Arkansas. He was an industry leader and someone I greatly respected, even though I didn't always show it.

As a smart-ass kid growing up, I saw things a little differently back then. He was a boss, so I was going to be a boss, too. I'd own my own company someday, just like him. I always loved to come up with ways to make money. I had paper routes, mowed yards, fertilized lawns, and I loved to buy and sell stereos and other items to make extra cash.

Dad was the general manager and majority shareholder at his company, which ran grain elevators in town, a barge-loading grain elevator on the Mississippi, a fertilizer plant, and a farm supply store. I wanted to be just like him and run a thriving business.

His operation was successful, and he had a great relationship with the bank. He'd go to the bank every year, sit across from the bank president and tell him how much money he'd need for the year to cover the cash flow for the receivables generated from buying grain for his grain elevators. Farmers had their own cash flow problems and would sometimes need to get paid before they delivered their crop—and certainly before his company got paid by whatever company bought the grain that was ultimately shipped down the river to New Orleans. Dad would stand up and shake the banker's hand, and the deal was struck. I took it for granted that that was how all business owners worked with their bank. It would take me decades to get to the same relationship with our bank.

I was an awful student in high school. I took all the hardest college prep classes, but I didn't care about grades. I used to joke that I graduated in the top two-thirds of my high school class. I got kicked out of school for a week during my senior year for supplying liquor to my classmates during an overnight Key Club meeting in Little Rock. A girl I knew in Little Rock came by the auditorium where the meeting was being held and took me and a couple of buddies out to find a liquor store before the meeting got underway. Our absence was noticed. Luckily, they couldn't prove we bought the liquor, so instead of being kicked out of school, we got suspended.

The next fall, it was time to leave home to start my freshman year at the University of Arkansas in, of course, the College of Business. Many of my friends had parents and family members weep and hug them when they left for school. My father, however, took a different tack.

He said, "Okay, jaybird, I'll see you again in six weeks after you flunk out."

His reverse psychology worked. I got two part-time jobs working in the cafeteria, even though I didn't need the money, and made the dean's list just to prove I could do it.

I worked for Dad's company every summer break doing grunt work that they saved up for my brother and me during the school year. Among the nasty jobs I performed, one particularly memorable one was shoveling rotten soybeans out of the elevator pits while rats hid in the corners. The rotten soybeans and scurrying rats made my autumn trek back to college especially welcome.

Dad didn't suffer fools, which is probably one of the reasons we didn't get along too well when I was younger. I was the typical know-it-all kid, too smart for my own good. But I did occasionally learn a lesson or two. I remember once when I visited Dad in his office and gushed, "You are so lucky to be the boss. I want to be the boss someday because then nobody can fire me."

"That's where you have it wrong," Dad said. "When you're the boss, everyone can fire you. If I don't do my job, the customers can fire me and trade somewhere else. If I don't treat them right, the employees can quit. And if I'm careless with their money, the banks can call my loans."

I tried to keep that lesson in mind when I started my own business—that and the idea that with great power comes great responsibility.

Dad would go nuts when someone made stupid small talk. Once he politely, but firmly, asked some nurses to hold the friendly, mindless banter when he was in the emergency room with an injury. They were just trying to be friendly, but he wasn't one for idle chitchat.

But then there was the time a guy dressed in rags came up to Dad outside his office and started to talk to him. I couldn't believe how calm Dad was as he stood there and listened to this man prattle on incoherently.

Afterwards, I asked, "Dad, why didn't you just dismiss that guy and move on?"

He replied, "That man was born that way and can't help who he is. There but for the grace of God, go I."

That was a lesson about humanity and humility that I would not forget.

As much as I admired my dad, I knew I couldn't work for him long term after college. In those days,

I was a liberal long-haired kid, and he was a buttoned-up conservative. I wanted out of our little backwater town and a chance to prove myself to the world.

After graduating from college, I worked one last late-spring wheat season for Dad's company while I waited for a job offer from one of the companies I'd interviewed with at school. I finally heard from the JC Penney Catalog Distribution Center about a management trainee position in their transportation department in Milwaukee, Wisconsin. This was in July 1976, and I was offered a salary of something like $9,000 a year. These were in the days before the Internet and Amazon, and people ordered out of catalogs. It was my first job after getting a bachelor's degree in business administration with a major in marketing and transportation. I had to look on a map to see where Milwaukee was. I'd never been north of St. Louis.

Even though we were called *management* trainees and had to wear coats and ties to work, our job was to learn the business. My specific title was traffic analyst, and I went through several months of training to learn various areas of the transportation department. We were responsible for coordinating the transportation of the product into the huge distribution center, as well as the outbound shipments to the stores and directly to the customers. Part of my training consisted of auditing freight bills, and I found I had a knack for recognizing mistakes.

I met the love of my life while in Milwaukee, the former Christine Reiter from South Bend, Indiana. Chris and I were attracted to each other like magnets from the start. Like me, Chris's first job after school was in

Milwaukee, where she worked as an interior designer with the most upscale furniture store in the area. Chris was a beautiful person inside and out then, and she still is, almost forty years later.

After dating only a couple of months, we told Chris's parents that we wanted to get married in five weeks. We had talked about moving to a warmer climate, and we wanted to get married before we moved. We said our vows in February 1978 and began to plan our escape from the harsh winters of Milwaukee.

Having grown up in the snowy winters of Indiana, Chris was used to the cold and snow, but the months of snow on the ground were more than this Arkansas boy could take. We talked about moving somewhere warmer, but I hadn't seen much of the country other than the states that surrounded Arkansas. Chris had been to Arizona as a teenager to visit her cousins in Paradise Valley and had good memories of her visit. I'd never set foot in Arizona, but the thought of a fresh start in the old West sounded pretty good to me, so we went for it.

I called a guy in Mesa, Arizona. I was told he did post-audits of JC Penney's freight bills, and I asked my prospective boss if he thought I could eventually make $20,000 a year auditing those freight bills. It was straight commission work, and he said he thought it would be possible. So a month after we married, we loaded up a U-Haul truck with our meager belongings, hitched Chris's car behind the truck (I sold mine to help pay for the move), and hit the road. We arrived in Arizona with a few hundred dollars in our pockets and a desire to create a better life for ourselves.

After we stayed with Chris's aunt and uncle a few days, we got an apartment in Scottsdale and paid the complex almost all the money we had left for rent and deposits. I still remember when my Aunt Toni sent us a late wedding gift of $100 and said to buy something we'd never forget. We bought groceries, and we never forgot! I know $100 doesn't sound like a lot of money now, but it helped us survive until our first paychecks arrived.

The auditing job was absolutely mind-numbing. I reviewed piles of freight bills retrieved out of stacks of boxes filled with thousands of others just like them. I'd put in a full day at the office looking for errors. At night, I worked as a doorman at TGI Fridays where Chris waitressed until she could land a design job. I made $16 a night for around five hours' work. The best part of the job was the free meal we got at the end of our shifts.

In my day job, I made 20 percent of any savings found, after the trucking company that had overcharged our client reimbursed the difference. As you can imagine, the trucking companies were in no hurry to pay our claims and would often deny them unless we had plenty of proof. It was hard work, but I enjoyed the challenge. It took a while to get things going, but after six weeks, I got my first commission check. I think it was for $33. Two weeks later, the check was for twice that amount: $66. Woo-hoo! But I wasn't discouraged; I knew upfront what the deal was. I was an independent contractor, so I got no salary, no benefits, and no guarantees.

Soon, however, the checks were good enough to quit my night job. I took boxes of freight bills home with me at night and put in twelve- to fourteen-hour workdays. Even though there were no guarantees, I liked that the harder and smarter I worked, the more money I could make.

I remember one night when I worked my way through a huge stack of freight bills in our apartment complex's laundry room. While clothes spun in the washer and tumbled in the dryer, I found errors totaling $4,000 (worth $800 to me, or what I'd made in a month at my old job). And we got a couple of loads of clean clothes done at the same time. Not too many jobs give you the opportunity to directly influence your income in what would normally be your spare time.

Eventually, the checks grew, and, as an independent contractor, I always set aside savings and money for the IRS in separate accounts. My first decent year, we owed the IRS so much that if we'd been able to keep it instead, we could have paid cash for a new Corvette. The thought that with a wife and growing family, the IRS took enough from our pockets to purchase a car of that magnitude didn't seem fair.

I still don't think it's fair. Today, we have to fund inventory and accounts receivables, which we haven't gotten paid for, and still the IRS counts it all as income. Some years, I've had to take out huge loans to cover tax bills in the millions. When you hear about the greedy 1 percent who pay a lower tax rate than their secretaries, they're not talking about the small business owner who's trying to fund his company and yet, has to pay out 40 percent of accruals in taxes. Your net worth goes up, but when you have to borrow money to pay taxes, it's the worst. The only thing worse is if you don't need to pay taxes because your business lost money.

The next year, still with a bitter taste in my mouth from the previous year's tax bill, I swore we wouldn't pay the IRS as much and looked for any legal ways to lessen their take. We bought a few income properties to see if that would help; in those years, the tax laws for income property were pretty favorable. It did help us pay less in taxes, but the primary reason was because at first, we lost money as the mortgage payments exceeded what we took in as rent. Dad tried to warn me that there were people who did real estate investing for a living, and we were at a disadvantage, but we tried it anyway. Not a great idea. I hated being a landlord.

So the following year, we refocused on a better way, and we started to look at absentee businesses–that is, a business that runs itself with a manager, and you don't have to be present every day. We looked at a few offerings and decided to buy a daycare center. It was in a low-income part of town, but I liked the low overhead and the fact that most of the moms were government subsidized.

Chris doesn't like the term "absentee," and she'll tell you that even though she didn't have to go in on a daily basis, she did have to interact with the director every day, even several times a day. The business was always on her mind. She knew nothing about how to run a daycare center before we bought it, but she made it work. This investment lost money at first, like almost everything new we tried, but the income that business generated eventually made it one of the pillars of our success.

In 1982, at age twenty-eight, I made $80,000 from the audit position, which was considered pretty good money back in the day. It seems unbelievable, but that income put me in the top 2 percent of earners. Even though my eyesight suffered from scanning freight bills over twelve hours a day, the income seemed to justify that sacrifice. Savings would be necessary to achieve our goals.

We had a small business, a house, and income properties. Then something unexpected happened.

I discovered my boss didn't like the fact that I made so much money. Even though he had no investment in me, and even though he profited from every dollar I saved our clients, he hired more people (I was his first contractor) and had them filter the bills before I got them. So that next year, I made $35,000, and I swore I'd never work for anyone else again. I made up my mind to quit the day before my thirtieth birthday, and I was able to do so because of the discipline of saving money, assembling assets, and owning an absentee business that generated cash flow.

I was incredibly angry about what my former boss had done to me, but I channeled that anger into a determination to become successful on my own. I wanted to control my destiny, and I was willing to take all the risk to get all the reward. I wanted no partners, because I'd heard too many horror stories about businesses being torn apart because the partners didn't agree, and I'd witnessed firsthand how counterproductive many partnerships become. I was also determined that I'd never cut any of my employees' legs out from under them, simply because they made a lot of money. I knew any proper profit-sharing or commission plan would benefit our company and myself more than my employees, and, in turn, they'd stay motivated to do even more.

My job had served its purpose. I'd saved enough money to afford to quit, and I'd learned I couldn't work for someone who didn't care about the welfare of his people. So I took a couple of days off to plan our next move and started to look for businesses that I could afford to buy and that had the potential to grow.

If you've ever shopped for a business, you've probably found plenty of bad, low-income businesses for sale. I figured if I was going to work my butt off in my own business, I should buy one with the upside potential for a decent income. Chris wasn't thrilled with my early retirement, and after I'd looked for just three weeks at only a couple of prospects, she suggested I pull the trigger on one, get out of her hair, get a job, and get out of the house.

Because I had a degree in transportation, I selected a small airport cab company, which looked much better on paper than it truly was. I thought, *How hard could it be?* Well, it was harder than I ever imagined.

Lessons Learned

- Becoming a business owner is relatively easy; running a business is another story.
- People from all walks of life own businesses, but only a few excel.
- If you aren't fully prepared to be a business owner, you can overcome it.

2

No One Teaches This Stuff

My anger at my old boss served as the catalyst for me to buy a business as soon as possible. I used to vilify the guy for his greed, but then I ran into him several years later at a Denny's restaurant.

He walked up to our table and said, "Remember me? I'm your old boss, and now I see your cars everywhere. Seems like you've done pretty well."

I said, "Yes, we've been real fortunate. What have you been up to?"

He stared at me with a dead look in his eyes and told me that he had nothing. "My wife left me, and my kids are grown and have cut ties with me. The business is gone." He said that to fill his idle time, he took solo motorcycle road trips.

I thought to myself, *What a sad life. This guy could have had it all.*

When I remembered the way he'd treated me when I worked for him, and how he'd treated others, it made me think that maybe we really do reap what we sow. I always think of his experience as one of those examples that illustrate that bad behavior begets bad results.

I actually owe that man a debt of gratitude because he set me on the path to business ownership at a younger age than most. Over the years, I've met many qualified people who wanted to start their own business. But they were too far down the road with a family or a good job with benefits, and they didn't want to take the kind of risk that comes when you buy or start a business. In other words, they were trapped by their own success. When my old boss wrecked my income, he set me free to try something, *anything*, other than to continue to work for him.

There are a few exceptions to this rule. Jeff Bezos, the founder of Amazon, had a lucrative career at a Wall Street hedge fund. He told his boss about his idea to open an online bookstore. His boss told him that sounded like a good idea for someone who didn't have such a good job and encouraged him to sleep on it for forty-eight hours. Bezos, of course, decided to do it, even though he had to turn his back on a great career and forfeit his annual bonus. He couldn't give up on an idea he thought would plague him with regret later in life if he didn't take his best shot.

Anyone can start or purchase a business, but not everyone will make the sacrifices or have the discipline to make it work. There are a lot of reasons that eight out of ten small businesses fail. The odds are stacked against you. You have to learn so much in so little time. The sellers will always take your money, but you have to learn the ins and outs needed to run that particular business in that particular industry.

There are no shortcuts to success, but I learned that you can put the odds to work in your favor. Working the odds isn't the same as playing the odds. We lived in Phoenix for nearly twenty years before we took a trip to Las Vegas because, even though I had a large appetite for risk, I liked to play only when our team and my own actions could help control the outcome. I didn't want to depend on Lady Luck.

Back in the seventies, the College of Business at the University of Arkansas focused, like most business schools, on turning out management employees for big companies. The curriculum focused on compliance and rules and regulations, not innovation. They didn't have courses for students interested in developing new and better ways to do a job. None of the classes I took addressed how to start your own business or entrepreneurship.

By the time my son, Jacob, was a student at the University of Notre Dame, they offered degrees in entrepreneurship, which ended up as his major, but they still didn't get into the nuts and bolts of how to get a company out of the blocks, down the track, and racing toward victory. I think this is one of the main reasons Harvard Business School requires MBA candidates to work for a couple of years before they enroll. They know that to succeed, you have to understand the context and realities of business, not just textbook theories.

This lack of preparation is a huge challenge for anyone who wants to start or buy a business, or who inherits a family business. After all, how can you know how to proceed if you're not sure where you're going?

As a new business owner, you'll find yourself doing many functions that you never had to do before. And many times you—the business owner—will have no one else to lean on. We often find that we have to go on this journey almost singlehandedly. We have to learn to promote our business, balance the books, investigate regulations and laws that govern our operation, get the correct permits, handle taxes, manage cash flow and risk, navigate human resources, and more. Very little of this is covered in business school, and certainly not to the degree you must learn when you're going it alone.

Many business owners fall into this trap. You first have to learn every aspect and function in your business, and then you have to learn how to turn those functions over to someone more qualified than you to do them. Eventually, you'll find that your duties will take you full circle from doing or overseeing every job in the company, to finally settling in on your role as business owner. It's a role where you lead with vision, provide a high level of oversight, and let more qualified employees manage the business.

But not at first. When you first take over or start a business, you have to learn everything, including:

- How do you promote your business?
- What products or services will you sell?
- How do you make sure people want what you have to offer?
- What's your value proposition?
- Will you make money when you deliver your product?
- What do you know about the marketplace?
- What systems do you need in place?
- What do you have to do to be in compliance with the law?

There are so many questions, but where do you find the answers? Sometimes you don't know the answer until it's too late.

I learned a very valuable, but punishing, lesson the first year when I failed to pay the federal government the payroll withholding tax. We didn't have a profit yet, and I didn't take a salary. Money was short, so I stuck my head in the sand. I should have known better, because I used a payroll service at our other business, but I cut manual checks and had no idea how to file the payroll taxes. This oversight came home to roost the next year when I got a notice—and a fine—from the IRS.

This example shows why we must meet all of our problems head on. They won't go away if we ignore them. They'll only fester and get worse.

I read the notice and thought, *How am I going to pay all of these fines, interest, and tax payments and still keep the company running?*

There was no easy way. I immediately started to use the same payroll company Chris's daycare business used. Then I doubled down to find a way to get all of our tax payments resolved, so the company could keep going.

I threw myself into my work to try to create a better business. I even went so far as to drive a cab on busy Fridays. I'd be out doing last minute PR work at the bars on a Friday afternoon, then go back to the office and see calls that hadn't been covered. I worked until the backlog cleared, and it gave me a good idea about how much money our drivers could make and whether we had enough cars on the road. I also got to talk to our customers and gauge how they liked our service and what could be improved. I liked the reward I got when I promoted our company at new and different locations and then, on returning to the office, saw the first-time calls those new locations generated.

Find Guidance

Because of the Internet, business owners can easily access more advice than ever before, but not every "expert" is truly an expert. I recommend that you take advice from someone who has actually worked in the trenches and created a successful business, rather than from a consultant to a successful business. It would be worth your time and effort to get a recommendation or check references. While there are some very knowledgeable consultants, many more consultants consult because they couldn't succeed on their own. We've all heard the expression, "Those who can, do; those who can't, teach." While not always true, it often is.

Although there's much more information available, the game is changing faster and faster. What worked yesterday won't necessarily work tomorrow. Current and future disruption has every industry under attack. Today, everyone carries a computer in his or her phone. Artificial intelligence programs have made great strides. And we've already seen that cars will soon be self-driving! Our world is changing rapidly, and not in a linear fashion, but rather in a quantum way. Yet we're still linear beings and build our businesses day by day.

> What worked yesterday won't necessarily work tomorrow. Current and future disruption has every industry under attack.

This means you can't just *talk* about changing your model; you have to actually *do* it. And then you have to constantly reevaluate and constantly improve, day after day.

I attended a lunch presentation at the Arizona Biltmore, and the ballroom was full of mergers and acquisitions professionals, as well as C-level executives. The CEO of a company I was very familiar with gave a presentation. He said that even though their business was XYZ, they considered themselves to be a technology company because that was where their future was. The audience thought he was right on and had made a great point. But because of what I knew about their operation, I knew he was just *talking* about what they needed to become because their technology was actually woeful. They weren't *doing* the hard work or making the investment needed to change that reality.

Just because we say something, that doesn't make it true, and telling these lies to others *and to ourselves* won't substitute for the effort we need to exert to keep our companies relevant.

Although you have little choice but to learn every aspect of your operation firsthand, so you're in the loop and better prepared down the road, there are other sources of wisdom than the school of hard knocks. I read many of the business books that were available in the eighties and nineties. One of my favorites is *Customers for Life* by Carl Sewell. Sewell created a terrific business by taking care of his employees and constantly exceeding his customers' expectations.

I was also fortunate to have my dad as a positive role model because he ran his business with integrity and high morals. There were also reverse role models from a couple of business owners I'd worked for who taught me how *not* to treat employees and vendors.

You will make mistakes, but you will learn from those mistakes, and it will make you a stronger owner in the long run.

So again, where does a business owner find answers? In the early days, I may have been too proud to ask others for their advice because I didn't want to admit that I couldn't do it on my own. So I read a lot of business books, and every book offered a different insight on how to become a better business owner. I never asked others in my industry how to run a company, because I didn't want them to know how little I knew. Instead, I gleaned a lot of information from those I came in contact with every day, and I filtered their advice, knowing it came from their point of view. These were people who applied for a job with us, and if they had worked for someone else in the industry, I peppered them with questions and then listened and processed their responses. I got some great insights from this method, insights and perspectives that many business owners don't seek out, but I wouldn't recommend it as your only learning tool.

It wasn't until we were in business for almost twenty years that I joined Vistage, a CEO peer group. The thing I liked most about Vistage was that we met monthly with other CEOs whose businesses were at various stages. Some folks could help me solve a problem because they had resolved the same problem in the past, and many heads are always better than one. It was like getting a CEO degree, which was more useful than getting an MBA.

I participated for seven years and got a lot of help to grow our company to ten times the size it was when I started. I thought so much of the experience that we got several of our higher-level people involved in Vistage groups, and they are still involved to this day.

There are also associations you can join both locally, like the Small Business Association, as well as national industry groups where you can talk with people who have already gone through what you face. I could have saved myself some headaches and learned some of the basics through people who ran larger transportation companies all over the country. However, I tend to think that some of our success was based on the fact that we didn't know what we were doing, so we could go in any direction we wanted. We weren't stuck in an industry mindset that there is only one way to do this. If we had developed that mindset, we would have never evolved to be the successful company we are today.

To own a business is a journey of self-discovery. Before I bought mine, I didn't know if I was a good or bad manager because I had never managed anyone before. I had all these jobs that had to be performed that I knew nothing about, but I had to learn them. I didn't know how to hire or fire anyone. I didn't know the proper way to keep books. I didn't know the most effective way to promote our business. I didn't know anything about how to buy vehicles, how to properly maintain them, or how to dispose of them when they got old.

How would I? I'd been a management trainee and then an auditor of freight bills before I bought a business–not a very practical path to entrepreneurship. What I'm saying is that I had no special training or background. So what we were able to do with a small, underperforming business is something anyone should be able to do.

There was an ace in the hole, if you want to call it that. I had faith in my ability to succeed, and so did Chris. She always gave me her full support. I may have been somewhat delusional and naive, but I truly believed I couldn't fail. I wouldn't *allow* our company to fail. We would figure it out. And on the occasions that we did fail, we usually failed small and not in a way that would put us out of business.

Looking back, we did things that felt like we were being loyal to our employees, but these actions actually held the company back. We had a promotion process that we now call "selecting the tallest of the dwarfs." When we needed a new manager or supervisor, we didn't take the time to hire the best person for the job. We took the fast and easy approach and awarded the fastest phone operator or longest-term employee with that promotion. That's the lazy way out, and we did it for longer than I like to admit before we changed our policy to make the best hires, no matter where we had to find them.

> I had no special training or background. So what we were able to do with a small, underperforming business is something anyone should be able to do.

So how did I learn what I was good at, what I was bad at, what I liked to do, and what I didn't like to do? Owning a tiny business and wearing a lot of different hats sorted out those questions in no time.

Some decisions were easy to make. I knew nothing about mechanics or how to maintain vehicles so, of course, we hired a mechanic. I watched what he did and learned a little by osmosis. When you spend your own money to pay for repairs, you soon learn how to troubleshoot simple problems to keep your costs to a minimum. That doesn't mean I was any good as a shop manager or that I enjoyed it, but that the kernel of knowledge helped me hold my ground when others were hired to manage the shop. I had to do jobs that I didn't enjoy and wasn't good at, but I acquired a knowledge for the work that was priceless. Someone had to answer our phones twenty-four hours a day and dispatch the calls to our drivers. And someone had to hire, train, and manage all those drivers.

I tried to manage the drivers at first, but it was different from my interactions with the people I grew up with. I'd ask drivers to behave a certain way, like pay their leases on time or bring their cars in clean, but they had a million excuses why they couldn't do it. I thought I had them figured them out, when I finally got so frustrated that I dropped a few F-bombs, and things changed. Their ears perked up, and they acknowledged that they'd heard what I said. I didn't really curse before this, but I got pretty good at it after I saw it got results.

One day, a new driver pulled some kind of boneheaded mistake, and I asked him to come into my closet-sized office to talk with me.

"What the hell did you think you were doing?" I asked. And then I continued to dress him down and let the F-bombs fly.

Suddenly, the guy started to cry and said, "You don't have to cuss at me like that."

I felt like a total jerk and thought, *What kind of monster have I become?*

That's when I figured out that I didn't have what it takes to manage people. I soon hired a guy with management experience to manage our drivers. I called him my "no" man. Small business owners are optimistic, and they tend to say "yes" to everything and everyone. I know I was like that and probably still am. If a guy came to me and wanted an extension on his lease until the next day, my usual answer was, "Sure." The drivers took that as a sign of weakness.

I told the new manager that he was responsible to keep the drivers away from me and to say "no" when they asked for favors. Well, he was a natural at that. He could tell a guy to go to hell, and the guy would thank him and be back at work the next day. He had the knack. I didn't. And when I tried, I failed, and I didn't enjoy it. That was a hat I was glad to surrender. You'll find that for every job you loathe to perform, there is someone who loves to do that precise thing and is ten times better at it than you'll ever be.

As I took off more hats, I used our managers as a shield. For instance, if a driver asked me for a favor, I directed him to the driver manager. "But you're the boss, and you can make whatever decision you want," he might say. I'd reply, "What kind of boss would I be if I usurped his authority and didn't let him make the decision?" It was important for me to assert the authority of our managers so that everyone knew that they were in charge of their departments.

I eventually figured out that I didn't like conflict and that there were plenty of others who were much better at it. I did like PR and promoting our business, but I couldn't do it full time. It was difficult for me to let go of the financial duties, as it is for most business owners. I believed that I had to approve every purchase and every dime spent and had to make sure that we had enough money to pay our bills. I wasn't going to fail, and so it was much more difficult for me to let that go. I know I wore some hats too long. There were so many people better equipped than me for these duties, but I hadn't yet given anyone that level of trust.

You have to start somewhere. The secret is to grow from there. When you're trying to get your business off the ground, no one tells you when to start and when to quit working. So many of us throw everything we have at the business and sometimes neglect the very ones we're trying to provide for. We have to take the time to set some limits and make a point of being a part of more in life than just the business. Your business will require your full attention and focus at times of change and stress, but that shouldn't be your standard operating procedure.

One way to say it is that you can't squeeze every nickel out of your business and still have a life. You can have a fulfilling business life and personal life if you impose some limits on your time with the business.

One time I had the brilliant idea to bring a scanner home so I could listen to our dispatch calls in the evening. I wanted to know where they originated. Chris pulled the plug on that idea right away.

> You can't squeeze every nickel out of your business and still have a life.

"Your office is for work," she said, "and when you're home, you need to interact with our family."

Lesson learned!

I didn't let our business cause me to miss important times with the kids. I attended all their games and special events that parents with nine-to-five jobs–who didn't have the flexibility to leave work during the day–couldn't attend. I let my flexible schedule work for me, which resulted in a great family life, even if I had to cover those missed hours some other time.

Your business may not give you the freedom to be that flexible. If you can't balance work with your home life, you have to fix that problem as soon as possible. When you get to the point that you can hire an additional employee, you'll find that you'll gain this precious freedom. If you don't have the freedom to live a happy life, that should be one of your first goals.

Will you make less money while you make this transition? Yes, but it's only temporary, and it will get you accustomed to building your business until *it* starts to work for *you*.

One thing I hear a lot from owners of new business startups is, "My business is too small, and I don't make enough to hire a manager." In that case, your number-one priority has to be to build your business until it can support hiring someone to help you. And if you hire correctly, this person will actually make your enterprise a lot more money than they cost you, and you'll be much happier as a result. This will unburden you enough to have the time you need to make appropriate plans to take your business to the next level again and again. That's when you start working *on* your business, not *in* it. You win, your family wins, and your business prospers.

Lessons Learned

- Every day, people start or purchase their own businesses, but it's difficult to find clear guidance about how to run a new business successfully.
- You have to learn to balance your home life with your work life.

3

Embrace Your Ignorance

When you buy or start a new business, there are tons of people who probably know more about that industry than you do. There are also people who are experts in every function you have to perform. It's wise to get as much feedback and information as you can from people who have different perspectives. You then have to filter that information through your own standards because we all have our own prejudices and filters. Try to read between the lines to gather the information you need. Can you take their ideas and tweak them into something new and brilliant? Should you dismiss everything that comes out of some veteran's mouth?

I remember a conversation with a guy who had been a cab driver for years. He told me that a night driver could afford to pay only a certain amount to lease a vehicle. I listened to his reasons but then filtered his comments with what I knew, and I was able to raise the cab leases because our business allowed us to. We never increased our meter rate or raised leases without doing the math to make sure our drivers did better than we did.

Don't be afraid to try something counter to an expert's advice if your gut tells you it's the right thing to do. If you go too far, you'll soon figure that out.

I had one particularly productive day very early on. I was sitting in the smoke-filled office that we shared with our operators and dispatchers, when a guy strolled in uninvited. We had about four months' experience in the cab business, and it was a real struggle to make ends meet. As a matter of fact, we had already racked up about $20,000 in losses in that short amount of time. It was apparent that we needed to change our model to be sure our drivers made enough money, so they could afford to pay our lease without a problem.

This guy heard what we were doing and said he wouldn't help me for free, but for a price (salary) he could teach me the ropes. I didn't know this guy from Adam, but I was smart enough to know he probably knew more than I did. He wrote his salary requirement on a piece of paper and pushed it toward me. I looked at that number and thought, *This will never happen, because I can't afford to put him on the payroll.* Hell, I couldn't even pay myself back then.

This guy wasn't a successful businessman, but he did have experience, and he absolutely knew how to promote a taxi business. Even though we couldn't pay him what he asked for, I sat there and let him talk. Over the next two hours, he couldn't help but show off how smart he was. He told me everything I needed to know to start a new street cab division and get it off the ground.

Sometimes it really pays to just keep your mouth shut and let yourself be educated. This guy wasn't very presentable, and he wasn't the type of person I wanted in our organization. But I didn't let that cloud my appreciation of his insight. Most of what he said turned out to be spot on. The one thing he didn't get right was his opinion that the name of the company wasn't important. After he finished talking, I thanked him for his time and let him know we just couldn't afford him.

Fairly soon after that meeting, we started a street cab company named Discount Cab. In a business like the taxi industry–where high prices keep people from using your services, or they use you only because it's a necessity and not a choice–that name was like magic. We put a slogan on the back of every car: We discount the price, not the service. People got it, and we delivered. I enjoyed promoting our service, and our call count quickly grew. We finally had some control over our destiny, and we started making a little money.

I had ridden in a cab only twice in my life–and never in Phoenix–before I decided to buy a cab company. I had to be one of the most industry ignorant people to ever buy a cab company. I had no knowledge of the business, but I didn't have any preconceived notions either. It's like my ignorance set me free. We didn't have to be like every other cab company, because I didn't even know what that meant.

I almost took that outsider perspective too far. Even though I knew there was a national association for taxi business owners, I was hesitant to join because I thought I had all the answers. Do yourself a favor. If there are groups you can join to increase your knowledge, join them if you can. You can still go down your own path, but you'll be better equipped to handle the job.

Too Expensive or Not?

A heavy expense in the cab business is car repairs. I could barely change my own oil, but I had to learn this part of the business before it broke me.

After watching a new low-wage mechanic break a bunch of parts and make a mess of things, I told the shop manager about the guy's poor work. I was shocked that he bragged about how low the guy's pay rate was. I estimated that the guy cost us three times his rate in shoddy work that had to be redone. I told the shop manager we couldn't afford to hire a mechanic who would work that cheaply. He got the message.

We had a similar experience years later when we added computers to our operation. I found the cheapest place in town to buy them, but they were so prone to failure that we started to purchase them from a national provider. They cost more up front, but the failures went away. So did the time and money we'd wasted.

Another time, as I wandered around the repair shop, a mechanic told me how hard it had been for him to fix a charging system. He'd replaced the starter, alternator, and battery, but nothing worked. He then bragged that he'd finally found a corroded connection and cleaned it up, which solved the issue. What he didn't understand was that he'd just wasted over $200 of the company's money on unnecessary parts. We soon decided we couldn't afford this mechanic either.

These are the kinds of mistakes and money holes that can sink your organization if they go unchecked. That's why you'll want to devote some time every week to "management by wandering around," especially in those early days.

Those lessons taught us to hire good managers, supervisors, and technicians in our shops. We found it much more efficient to pay more for the right people so money wasn't wasted and equipment was properly maintained and serviced. It's true that you often get what you pay for, and that doing things to save money in the wrong ways will cost you much more in the long run. These are lessons that are hard to learn other than by going down the wrong path in the first place.

Doing things to save money in the wrong ways will cost you much more in the long run.

When you first start your business, it's important to get feedback about how the customers perceive your product and how your employees feel about the company. This is easy information to get once you're established and have a budget for customer surveys.

We used a variety of inexpensive methods in the early days. Sometimes I'd drive a cab for few hours at a time to understand what our drivers experienced and to find out firsthand how happy our customers were. We also had employees and their family members become "mystery shoppers." They tested out our services, filled out a questionnaire, and reported back to us. If they turned in a completed questionnaire and told about their experience from the time they called for a cab until they were dropped off, we would comp their ride. They also reported if our team was rude or polite, if our service was prompt or late and, most important of all, if we'd delivered on our service promise.

Once we began hiring better talent, we didn't want to lose them, so we started conducting exit interviews to find out why an employee wanted to leave. Often it was because of their supervisor, in which case that information could be used to coach and evaluate supervisors and managers. I think a lot of small business owners believe they know what's going on better than they actually do, and exit interviews can really open your eyes.

These different forms of feedback helped us stay on the path we set out on—to create customers for life.

Lessons Learned

- Pay attention; you never know where your best ideas will come from.
- Make it a priority to first learn the parts of your business that could break you if you don't understand them.

4

Assess Your Current Situation

People go into business for a variety of reasons. Some join an established family enterprise after a long period of planning and training. Others inherit a business after a parent dies and are suddenly thrust into the role with no preparation. Still others start a business because they can't find a job or they're raising kids and want to work around their personal schedule. They might start selling items on eBay, Amazon, or Etsy, for example. Others have an idea they think is so good, they create a business to support it.

> A business doesn't become real until it produces enough margin that you can hire employees and have them work for you, while you focus on the growth and improvement of your operation.

Small business owners often want to make a better income than they could by working for someone else. But while they might make a decent living, too often they can't live the life they imagined because their business overwhelms them. It consumes them, *owns them*, instead of the other way around. The business owns their time and attention, and they lose the balance they need to live a meaningful life.

It's important to check your expectations and measure them against some common myths about business ownership.

Myth #1—I'll be my own boss, and nobody can tell me what to do.

Remember when I was young, and I told my dad that he was lucky because no one could fire him? He told me that if he didn't do his job, his customers could fire him and go to the competition, his employees could quit, and his banks could call his loans. When you go from working for someone else to working for yourself, you go from answering to one boss to answering to everyone—and being responsible for their success.

Myth #2—I'll let other people do all the hard work and then reap the rewards.

Someday that may be true, but to get to that level, your business will require all of your energy and attention. The good part is that because you're working on your dream, you'll want to work twice the hours you once worked for someone else. You'll actually want to work harder because you'll be eager to learn every role, and you'll be gratified to know that when you create new opportunities, you and your family will profit directly from that hard work.

Myth #3—I'll work the hours I want and take as many vacations as I can afford.

Really? Maybe you'll someday be that guy on the golf course at ten o'clock in the morning every

Tuesday, or you'll post Facebook updates of your snorkeling adventures from the Turks and Caicos islands. But before you get your business to that level, it will probably be more important to attend your kids' ballgames and put as much focus into your business as time allows. That's because the more successful your business becomes, the more it pulls you forward, and the more freedom it creates for you further down the line. The discipline you put into your business in the early years will pay dividends later, so you can be that guy in the snorkeling mask.

Myth #4–Owning my own business will make me rich.

ALERT: No one works with you because they want to see you get rich. No. They give you their time (employees) or their money (customers and investors) because they believe in you and what your company delivers. You'll make money because you solve problems. You'll grow your profits and your company because of the service you provide. You'll become a respected member of the community because you work to make it a better place.

The rewards will come when your customers recognize the difference your company makes in the marketplace. Customers and suppliers want to work with business owners who aren't in it just for the money. They want to work with business owners who are trying to make a positive impact in the industry and in the community. And they'll reward you for it. In fact, a positive, service-oriented attitude will be very profitable for you in the end because your customers become your evangelists.

The idea of owning a business is much more romantic than the reality of working in it. I've seen people buy sandwich shops so they didn't have to report to a boss. Then they found out it was a small-margin business that required them to stand on their feet all day and deal with customers. Turned out it was a lousy job and certainly not a real business. A business doesn't become *real* until it produces enough margin that you can hire employees and have them work for you, while you focus on the growth and improvement of your operation.

Even though these myths can deceive new business owners, they can also create a vision and a lifestyle you can work toward as you move your business forward.

Do you have what it takes to own a business? Ask yourself these questions:

- Are you truly an entrepreneur?
- When you were young, did you look for different ways to make a buck, or did you get excited to work for someone else?
- Do you have a high risk tolerance?
- Do you want to build a complex business that takes on today's challenges, or do you want a good job with guaranteed pay?

If you don't think you're suited to run a business or you don't have the desire to do so, there are plenty of places that would love to hire you, and you'll have peace of mind.

But if you think you have the right stuff and answered "yes" to the questions above, you still might be facing some roadblocks to success. Consider these:

- Is your business undercapitalized?
- Do you have partners who take advantage of you and stifle the business? The strife that comes from a partnership can easily upset what should be a good, profitable business.
- Did you buy a small business only to discover you really bought a bad job?

When I bought my business, I really thought I had what it took to own a business. But it was hard to be proud of that business and even harder to see a future in it. So I told myself, *It's not where you start, but where you end up that's important.*

It's not where you start, but where you end up that's important.

We recently hosted our trade group that held its convention in Phoenix. Most of the visitors were transportation business owners from across the country. They commented that they'd never seen such a professionally run organization, and that all of our "tour guides" (i.e., our employees) were knowledgeable and friendly. People come into our offices today and compliment us on the scope and professionalism of our operations and the attractive art on the walls, but it wasn't always this way.

Our first office was a cramped, uncomfortable, hazy smoke-filled office carved out of a dilapidated garage. There was only one room, and I shared it with two operators and a dispatcher, several of whom were hygienically challenged. I worked from a small desk next to the door to the bathroom. It was 1984, and it seemed like everyone smoked. Except me. I couldn't stand to be in that office for too long. We had a window air-conditioner that hummed valiantly, but it didn't do much with the acrid air.

Chris tried to dress up the office with an inexpensive mounted poster of a taxi that was covered with cellophane. The cellophane eventually got a hole in it, and the exposed part of the poster turned a dingy yellow from the twenty-four-hour-a-day assault of cigarette smoke. Not only was this company nothing to brag about, but we had to operate twenty-four hours a day, seven days a week, 365 days a year! It was definitely not sexy.

I wasn't proud to own it, and the employees weren't proud to work for it. So we decided to change it. To make it better. I put the business first, and we reinvested everything we made to get better vehicles and better facilities to make it easier to attract more customers and better employees.

At the end of our first year, we were in a space with much better offices, a nice repair facility, and a body shop. It wasn't the Taj Mahal, but it was quite a step up from that nasty first office. One of our primary goals was to put the facilities, infrastructure, and people in place that would allow the company to grow to the next level.

Even when you try your hardest, success can't be taken for granted. We were still in the first stage of the business cycle. Would we make it to the next cycle, or would we trip and fail?

Five Stages of the Small Business Life Cycle

If you decide you're in the right place and there's potential in your business, the next step is to determine where your business is in the business cycle, so you can set a strategy in motion to move to the optimal point.

Stage One: Startup

At this stage, the goal is to put the pieces together and get your business established. There's usually a lot of excitement and anticipation at this stage. You don't know if your business will be a success or not, but you work on your business plan, figure out what processes you need in place, and determine your cash flow needs. This can be an exhilarating time, but it's also the stage where most businesses fail. The pressure is always there, but if you have the necessary discipline, you can take your business to the next stage.

Stage Two: Growth

You've figured out enough to survive, and now you're ready to compete and win business. This is a fun, but trying, time. You must have a source of cash flow to help you through this stage because your business grows faster than the money flows. Much of the time, your company will be leaking oil, so you must keep a vigilant eye on all phases of the operation to keep failure at bay.

If you have the right systems in place, the cash will eventually catch up to fund even more growth. This is the period where too many entrepreneurs hit the wall. They have the sales, but they can't fund them. That's why cash flow is so critical. Make it past this stage, and the ride gets to be even more fun. Stall out, and your business could be on the way out.

This was when we started to put the odds in our favor. I noticed we had several different makes and models of vehicles, but one seemed better suited than the rest. Most of our fleet was manufactured between

1978 and 1982, a period that wasn't Detroit's finest moment. Cars were being throttled by smog control devices and computerized carburetors, and most weren't any good.

When we started to replace cars and grow our fleet, I chose the Ford Fairmont, an unremarkable but serviceable car, to be the standard vehicle for our fleet. The Fairmont was basically disposable, but it had a couple of features that really worked for us. Number one, it was cheap. I remember we got some for as little as $600. Two, it got good gas mileage around town. And three, it had a straight six-cylinder engine, which made repairs incredibly easy. I could buy a late-model wrecked Fairmont, and in just one day, our mechanics would use the parts from that wreck to trade out the interior, engine, transmission, and suspension to make a tired cab look like new.

I also decided on a paint scheme that made our vehicles stand out, and we installed decals on the cabs with DISCOUNT CAB emblazoned on the side in lettering as large as we could fit. Since the going rate for a Yellow Cab–at that time the largest fleet in the city–was $1.20 per mile, we put "90¢ per mile!" in large red lettering on the upper rear fenders.

We put clean cars on the streets with cents signs versus dollar signs, which really pushed our value proposition to the public. Of course, this would have done us little good if we didn't live up to our slogan, "We discount the price, not the service," posted in the rear window of every car. We grew that line from two vehicles to over thirty standardized vehicles over the next two years. Those steps helped move us forward with early growth.

Stage Three: Innovation and Expansion

Once you get through the growth stage, you must build a stronger organization. This is a heavy investment phase. You put your money into better facilities, equipment, and infrastructure, and you hire better talent to keep things humming. You may start to diversify your offerings so you can withstand a downturn in a segment of your operation. Just don't pursue new offerings until you nail down your primary business and it's earning enough money.

If you try too many things before you have the cash and support structure, you're doomed. Your growth should be rapid as you expand your footprint to multiple markets and diversified opportunities. In this stage, you can reinvent your company's products and stay ahead of the marketplace. I'll show you how we did this later in the book.

Stage Four: Maturity

In stage four, business is stable enough to withstand most unforeseen circumstances. You're probably making more money than ever before and are enjoying the ride. Where can your business go from here? There are usually a couple of options at this point. Option one is to take part of your business back to the expansion stage to make sure you stay relevant in the market. Option two is to exit by selling your interest. Option three is to sit there all fat and happy and move to stage five.

Stage Five: Decline—and Maybe Demise

You never want your business to hit this stage because it usually leads to demise. Some businesses are more stable than others, but if you don't pay enough attention, you may find that your industry is being disrupted and your business is no longer relevant. And worse, it's too late to reverse the decline.

Think about the difference between Blockbuster Video and Netflix. Blockbuster Video owned the lion's share of the after-theater, in-home video market. They cornered the market and raked in piles of cash—until they didn't.

While Blockbuster was enjoying its dominance, Netflix came in and offered videos by mail subscription. But Netflix really took off when it started to stream movies online. And the company continues to evolve and disrupt home entertainment, producing TV series and movies exclusively for Netflix viewers. This gives even more reasons for even more people to become customers.

Blockbuster was huge and could have had the foresight to reinvest, but it didn't. What's left now is a trail of empty stores. Avoid this stage of business at all costs. You must continually be on the outlook for new trends and experiment to stay relevant. Otherwise, the business dies.

Be careful. If you make the wrong moves, you can reach Stage Five from any of the other levels. The best place to be is Stage Four, producing a comfortable margin. But if you want a successful future, you must have a part of your business—or maybe even the main focus of your business—always in Stage Three, where you reengineer and experiment with your operation. Then you can stay ahead of the pack and be ready to protect your business when disruption comes your way. The largest, most successful organizations continually reinvent themselves before a competitor does something innovative or disruptive that makes them vulnerable.

Today, the business environment moves and changes faster than at any other time in history. You can be part of that change and stay ahead of the next wave of innovation or disruption. Or you can fall behind and get crushed by that same wave. It's your choice.

Lessons Learned

- Your first task is to get your sales to the point that you can afford to hire someone to help you.
- No one owes you success. It's up to you to attract it.
- No business is too small or so restricted that it can't morph into something much greater than it currently is.
- You must figure out what stage your business is in and identify the steps you need to take to get to the next stage.

5

Sometimes the Right Choice is to Quit

What do you do if you size up your situation and decide you can't get unstuck—or even if you could, that's not how you want to invest your time and effort? For me, the answer was to go away somewhere to think hard about my situation.

The first question you need to answer is: Should I own a business at all? It's not meant for everyone. You have to have a high risk tolerance and be very motivated and committed to its success, or else you're working against your nature. This will probably make owning a business—any business—too frustrating.

After two and a half years in business, we were growing, but because I didn't know how to manage our insurance risk, we found ourselves in insurance hell and paid an unsustainable one-third of our income to insure our vehicles. I could literally feel the noose tightening around my neck! I certainly felt trapped by this situation.

Back then, I didn't realize that insurance companies go through soft markets, and when they want to expand their business, they drop their rates to do so.

They also go through periods when the markets go hard, and they're forced to pay all their claims and clean up their balance sheets. So they dramatically raise their rates, especially to bad risks like small cab companies.

I'd received an unsolicited purchase offer from a much larger competitor, but I wasn't sure if we should take it or really knuckle down and outgrow our problem. So what do you do when you're broke and have to make such an all-important decision? Go on vacation to the beach, of course! Chris and I went to Coronado Island for about three days to sort things out with our toes in the sand, ocean waves rolling in, and seagulls coasting on the air currents overhead. This was a total change of scenery from working all day in the blazing desert of Phoenix.

While lying on the beach, I tried to listen to my mind, my gut, and my heart to find the right path to take. It was rare for us to get away from the kids and the day-to-day grind. We wanted to enjoy ourselves, but we had work to do and a decision to make.

Chris and I discussed the possible scenarios, and I told her, "If we're going to make the cab business work, we're going to have to borrow a lot of money to get past this insurance crisis. Even then, there are no guarantees we'll be successful."

She said, "The purchase offer sounds like a great opportunity and the chance to move on to the next chapter."

That was my concern. I had no idea what the next chapter looked like.

"I feel like a failure at business ownership," I told her. "I'm not sure what kind of job I'm qualified to do with my lack of experience. And what job will pay enough to support our family?"

I agreed that the deal to sell sounded good, but people had warned me that the potential buyer couldn't be trusted. And again, I didn't know what other kind of work I was qualified to do.

This might surprise you, but when I realized that I hated what I was doing and had a good way out, I decided to sell. It was a way for me to escape the entrepreneur's trap and, in my case, insurance hell. Because we were in Stage One and were working on our growth objectives for Stage Two, there was opportunity to move forward, but there was also a lot of risk. I knew our business could go into decline and then demise at any point along the way.

Even though I decided to quit, it was in a positive way. Someone was going to pay me a lot of money for what we had created. But the people who warned me about the buyer were mostly right. He was a shrewd negotiator. When I told him I was ready to sell, he agreed to buy, and by then, I'd already mentally checked out of the business. But once we reached an agreement, he said couldn't give me the entire down payment and would have to pay it off over time. I was so checked out that I agreed, even though I negotiated a little better payment schedule than he originally proposed.

What happened after the sale was what surprised me. I never wanted to work for anyone again, which was why I'd bought a business in the first place. Plus, I hated the cab business. The buyer said he'd bought my business because he wanted me to work for him. I had done some creative things to move our company forward, and he liked that.

He had only one cab company, but in the Yellow Pages (remember those?) he'd listed a company for every community in the valley. I thought that was a great idea, and I decided to trump his listings. For example, right after his listing for "Scottsdale Cab" was our listing for "Scottsdale Discount Cab." Which one would you call? I told him I didn't want to work for him, but the offer was flattering. He was a persistent and persuasive guy, and after numerous discussions, I finally agreed to work as a consultant.

To my surprise, I found that once the weight of ownership was off my back, I really did enjoy working in and growing the business. It was a chance to see what it was like to operate a larger company and gain confidence that I could run a business that was much larger than what I'd had. After a year, he talked me into being the general manager rather than a consultant.

We had five-year buyout, and I worked with him for three and a half years. Then he went through an expensive divorce and declared bankruptcy, both personally and professionally. He offered to default on our agreement, which meant that he could either return the company to me or sell it to a competitor.

I decided to take the business back, even though the assets we'd brought into the original deal were gone, so I'd have to borrow money to start up again. But after the stint with his company, I was confident that I could not only start back up but also manage and grow the business. And we did. Less than six months after taking back our company, we bought out a troubled company and tripled our sales.

If you've given your business every chance, but you feel trapped and like there's no way out, the best solution may be to sell it–or shut it down if it's not salable–and find something else that has more growth potential. I was fortunate because I'd collected most of the money from the sale, and I received a hands-on, paid education in how to run a larger operation.

Most importantly, I learned how to manage risk. My old business actually had a lot more potential than I thought it did when we sold it.

The first thing I did was to take on some short-term debt, so I could buy equipment. But I made sure to maintain 100 percent ownership. I believe it's extremely important to retain as much ownership as possible.

Think the process through from the beginning. For example, that $25,000 you need to keep your company going might cost you 25 percent of your small company. That may not seem like a big deal at the time. After all, you need the money, and your business is worth close to nothing. But if you can turn things around and create a billion-dollar business over time, giving up your equity is the most expensive money you could ever get.

I remember a great example from *How to Get Rich* by Felix Dennis, the founder of *Maxim* magazine. Four or five of his top managers teamed up and issued him an ultimatum. Give them a total of 20 percent of the equity, they said, or they'd walk and start their own competing magazine. He fired them all on the spot and did all their jobs himself until he could replace them. Their new venture went bankrupt, while the 20 percent that Dennis retained was eventually worth $80 million. That would have been some expensive compensation.

Profit sharing is an excellent annual incentive device, but don't ever give up your equity. You take the risk; you get the reward. You fail; you fail. Don't fail.

Sometimes you have no choice, but there are lots of places to borrow non-equity money. Even if you have to pay a high interest rate, it might be worth it because you retain control of your future. When we got our business back, I got to press reset and start all over again, this time with much more knowledge than I had in the first place. It was up to me to take full advantage of the opportunity.

Before we sold the company, we didn't get very far into Stage Two of the small business life cycle, but this time would be different.

Lessons Learned

- Sometimes the odds aren't in your favor, and your best course of action is to find a way out and then refocus for your next venture.
- Giving up equity for cash is the most expensive and encumbered money you can raise.

6

How I Took Advantage of My Second Chance

When I was in high school, it seemed like I learned the lessons better if I got the answer wrong first. That didn't help my grade-point average, but I usually remembered the lesson and didn't get it wrong again. In business, as in life, you don't know what you don't know, and so it's almost impossible *not* to make mistakes. But making them can be a good thing because of the lessons they burn in your mind.

I think I did about everything wrong when I first got into business! It's amazing what I didn't know, and I was cocky enough to think I knew quite a bit. One of my early lessons was that people are more than willing to lie to you to keep their job.

I remember a driver from my first time around named Ray. Ray was an older guy and a real hoot. He told me he measured success not from his fares, but from the large tips he got when a delighted customer got out of his cab with a smile on his face because of the jokes and stories he had shared them with. I liked Ray; most everyone did.

One day, I got a report from a passenger that Ray smelled like liquor and was slurring his words. I had the dispatch unit find him and tell him I was on my way to see him.

It was late afternoon when I arrived at Ray's apartment. I told him about the complaint.

Ray looked at me and laughed. "You've got to be kidding; I would never drink and drive!" He walked over to his cupboard and retrieved a bottle of liquor and a jar of peanut butter.

"Listen, Craig, I'm off duty now. But if I wanted to drink and drive, I would do this, and no one would smell the alcohol."

"Do what?" I asked.

Ray took a shot of the liquor and downed it. He then swallowed a spoonful of the peanut butter.

He came over to me and breathed in my face. "Can you smell alcohol on my breath?"

"No, actually, I can't," I said.

Ray laughed and winked. "You see, I'm off duty and sober. Whoever reported me must have been having a bad day or they didn't like my jokes."

Satisfied, I thanked Ray for his time and went on my way.

But three days later, Ray caused a wreck and got a DUI. It should have occurred to me that anyone who knew how to hide the smell of alcohol on his breath probably had a drinking problem. Another expensive lesson learned.

Drivers who got in wrecks always told me they'd get their ticket thrown out because they weren't at fault. These bad drivers can put you out of business fast. They all wanted a second chance after a small wreck, but if I kept them on, that small wreck almost always led to a bigger one later on. And those larger wrecks were what put our company into insurance hell with excessively high insurance premiums. It took a while before I got the message that if I didn't manage risk, it could bankrupt us. It took me even longer to realize if we managed risk correctly, it would give us a competitive advantage.

We'll always have areas of our business that cause us pain. Our job is to improve outcomes to the point that the problem is fully addressed. Nothing feels better than putting a source of pain to work for you and turning it into a strength.

We'd flown a little too close to the sun our first time around, and I knew we couldn't afford to screw things up the second time. But that didn't mean we wouldn't stretch our little organization. When we got our business back, we had a small group of employees and drivers who believed in me and what we were trying to do, and they joined the effort. They believed that this time would be different. Instead of zero experience, I now had six years under my belt. I wouldn't let any "Rays" trip me up this time around.

We'd lost some of our former customers and drivers to smaller companies that had started up after our sale to the larger company, and we wanted to bring that work back. Most of those companies weren't well run and were ripe for the picking. I had very little cash, but the other companies didn't know that. I made them attractive offers to operate their cars on our fleet at a reduced rate and convinced them to turn their inbound calls over to us.

We probably did this with five small companies, and it worked out for a number of reasons. We didn't have the funds at that time to own all the vehicles ourselves, and they brought us their customers and drivers.

Six months later, we got wind that a company twice our size with double the calls had closed its doors and was selling its fleet. I contacted the owner as soon as I got the word and set up a meeting. He'd been doing a high volume of calls and really knew how to grow the business. The trouble was, he didn't have a clue how to run it. I struck a deal to buy his company assets on a payment plan, and I got him to forward his phone lines to us so we could start to service his customers. I also took over the lease on his facilities and purchased all his vehicles and equipment. I wasn't sure what we were getting into, but I didn't think we could go wrong.

Right after the purchase, I went on a short family vacation that we'd already planned and paid for. I should have backed out of the trip, but I couldn't send Chris on vacation with four small kids and no extra hands. When I got back, I found that it was a very expensive vacation. We were nowhere close to having enough management on board at this time to cover my absence. The former shop manager of the purchased company and some of his mechanics had absconded with a lot of the expensive shop equipment that we hadn't inventoried yet, and they'd set up their own independent repair shop. The vehicles that had come with the purchase were in terrible shape, and I had to have our shop manager hire new mechanics so we could fix or replace the fleet we inherited.

We had grown by 200 percent overnight, and our organization wasn't prepared to take on such a huge challenge. We had to operate two dispatch centers and two repair yards at first because neither was large enough to accommodate the combined staffs and fleets. We eventually got a facility that allowed us to combine dispatch and then found a repair center large enough to accommodate the combined fleets. It still wasn't an ideal situation. It would have been better to find a space large enough for our office and shop to be under one roof, but we didn't have time.

At first, we kept the other company's name because they had name recognition and a large following. But it didn't take long to find out why they'd closed their doors. They let anyone drive for them as long as the driver paid his lease, and they never ran a background check on a driver. When we put all their drivers through a background check, we had to let over half of them go for moving and criminal violations and hire new drivers to replace them.

Then we started getting a lot of calls from law firms looking for the previous owner. I took the calls and told the callers I was the new owner. Apparently, the company had several million dollars in judgments against it, and many of these law firms had judgments or claims against the previous owner. He'd never gotten around to forming a corporation and had been operating for three years with no insurance! It took a lot of my time to clear these claims, which they tried to attach to me. I was so glad that we'd purchased the assets of the company, not the company itself.

There are two ways to buy a company. An asset sale is exactly that: you buy the former owner's assets and good faith. Contrast that to a stock sale transfer, where you purchase all the rights and stock of the previous owner. You buy all the receivables and assets, and you also assume any liabilities.

One day, an attorney called me and said, "My firm has a million-dollar judgment against you."

I could tell from his tone that he was young and inexperienced. "Sorry, buddy," I told him, "but it was an asset purchase. You need to pursue the previous owner."

The former owner had, by the way, disappeared from the grid except on the day his payment from me was due.

The lawyer replied, "No, the claim is your responsibility."

I told him, "Listen, why don't you talk to your boss, tell him it was an asset sale, and see what he says?"

He called me back later and complained. "Well, that doesn't seem fair. You were right. Our claim is against the previous owner."

I thought I was smart, but a few months after the sale, I received a call from the Arizona Department of Revenue and got an education of my own. The official said the state had a lien on all the company assets. I told him that it was an asset sale, but he said it didn't matter because a tax judgment goes against the assets. The previous owner owed the state around $100,000 in back taxes, so the department had placed a UCC-1 filing against the company with the secretary of state. That was the first time I'd even heard of a UCC-1 filing.

I decided to call his bluff because I was so upset with the expense of all the broken-down vehicles we'd gotten. I told him, "Come get the cars. I don't even want them."

"We just want the money," he said.

I said, "Great, but I owe only $30,000 more to the seller."

"We need everything he owed us," he said.

"Well, you'd better come pick up the vehicles."

He eventually agreed to settle for the balance we still owed the seller. I told him we'd make the $10,000 monthly payments over the next three months, which was the same agreement I had with the former owner.

He said, "No, we need it all now."

"Then you'd better pick up the cars."

He finally agreed and said, "Okay, we'll take the payments."

It was one of the best negotiations I ever made because I didn't care if he took the cars. The real value of that company was the calls, and by then we'd already retired half of the worn-out cars we'd received in the deal.

About a week after we reached a settlement with the state, the seller slipped back into town from wherever he was hiding from bill collectors. It was time for him to collect his next payment–or so he thought. I told him about the lien by the state and that we'd agreed to settle for the balance of what was owed to him. He wasn't happy, but he knew he didn't have a leg to stand on. So he slid back under his rock, and I never saw him again.

It took us over a year to digest this deal, but about fifteen months after we closed it, we moved all of our operations into one incredible facility. We had the nicest cab facility in town, and we were now the third-largest cab company in the city. I'd lost a lot of hair during that ordeal, but we emerged stronger and were ready to move to the next phase. Or were we?

Lessons Learned

- We all make mistakes. It's how you recover that's important.
- Sometimes we negotiate best with our backs against the wall.

7

The Long, Slow Slog

We moved into our new facilities in December 1991. It was a recently updated 20,000-square-foot building on two paved acres. We'd negotiated a very favorable lease, and, by all appearances, we looked prosperous. The only problem was that I had to reinvest every dollar to keep moving forward, or sometimes to keep from going backward.

In order to accomplish this, we had to pull our company out of the Dark Ages. Our facilities were nice, and it always amazed me how much value people put on outward appearances. Prospective drivers would come into our lobby and ask us where the cab company was located. They thought they'd accidentally walked into a law office. Little did they know that I'd purchased all our nice furniture at auctions for pennies on the dollar.

I got to be the auction king for several years. I bought everything I could, including office furniture, art for the walls, and, of course, vehicles to keep our fleets up to date. I had two imperatives: it had to be high quality, and it had to be a bargain. I'd heard too many tales about owners who wanted to look like they'd made it, so they spent all their money to appear successful rather than using the money to move the business forward. The furniture I bought at auction was often what its first owner had bought new before he went bankrupt.

The appearance of success, however, did pay dividends. We had an insurance salesman who would compliment us on our facilities and tell us that we must be on our game. Then he'd give us discounts on our premiums. Vendors seemed eager to add us to their client list, and our nice shop made it easier to hire better mechanics.

My personal office was stupid big, something like twenty feet by thirty. I had a huge desk that had belonged to a bank officer before we bought it at auction. I also had glass cabinets to display my taxi memorabilia and a large sitting area that looked like a living room. We had an oversized lobby and conference room and very nice furniture.

I even started to buy into the "we must know what we're doing because it looks like it" mindset. But then I got a wakeup call that put it all into perspective. We'd just hired an experienced sales manager, and I invited him to our monthly managers meeting, which we held in our impressive conference room. All the managers reported what was going on in their respective areas and took questions.

After the meeting, I turned to the new guy and asked, "Well, what did you think?"

He didn't hesitate. "You have a nice group of employees and an open dialogue."

I beamed with pride. "Thanks!"

But then he popped my bubble. "That meeting reminded me of a country club meeting."

"What do you mean by that?" I asked, no longer so full of myself.

"Well, everyone got to talk and get his problems off his chest, and people felt better because of that. But there's no action plan, no scope or timeline to fix the problems. So how do you expect to improve your operation?"

I was crestfallen. My lack of experience couldn't hide behind our new offices, no matter how professional they appeared. We were missing pieces to the puzzle, and I had to figure out how to fix that. We needed to be as professional as our offices made us appear.

From the time I got into the taxi business until that point in the '90s, we had a manual dispatch system. Our call takers took the calls, wrote them down on little pieces of paper, and passed them over to the dispatcher. The dispatcher had a large board and sorted the calls by zone. He also logged the cabs by zone and assigned the calls to the closest cab using our private radio band. It wasn't very sophisticated, but that method had worked for decades for cab companies all over the world. However, our increasing call volume made it hard to manage all that paper. We needed to change.

It was time to enter the computer age. This would not be an easy transition because, at this time, we still employed people who'd worked in the cab business for years, and they were afraid of change. We finally found an inexpensive system that allowed the call takers to enter the trips into the system, and then the dispatchers would send the trips out over a pager system. The drivers still had to confirm by radio that they'd received the trip because the pagers operated in only one direction. If we had a glitch in the system, we had to revert to manual dispatch until we got it fixed.

In a very short period, we went from having no computers to practically everyone using one. We installed servers; had at least twenty-five computers in the call center; and acquired computers for the shop, for accounting, for risk management, and for cashiering. Eventually, every manager in the company had one.

We also had to purchase new phone systems and newer diagnostic tools for the shop to keep up with the more complex vehicle systems. So even though our income was slowly climbing, we were stuck at Stage Two, the growth stage. We weren't able to move on to Stage Three, innovation and expansion, because we'd simply come out of the Stone Age with the rest of the world.

We had to row as hard as we could so we wouldn't be swept back downstream. I knew that we didn't have all the pieces and that something was missing. In spite of that, we eventually reached $10 million a year in sales, but then our growth began to stall. I've read that 96 percent of small businesses never get past $1 million in annual sales. We'd been in business almost twenty years, but we still couldn't get out of Stage Two. Sometimes it felt like our only purpose was to pay the bills so we could live another day.

This is an important step in the progression of your business. You have to prove that you can pay the bills and that your company is worth the effort put in by your employees and outside partners and vendors. You can't skip this step, but you don't want to stay there so long that your progress stagnates. You need to move past this stage so you can innovate and expand. I wish someone had come along to shine a light on this issue years before we finally figured it out.

It wasn't like we didn't try. We'd bid on work outside our normal scope but wouldn't be awarded the work. There was something that our organization was missing, but I didn't know what it was.

Well, the problem was *me*. I didn't want to fail, so I made sure our vendors were paid on time, that we made payroll, and that we had the money to keep the operation running. But I was holding on so tightly that I missed the bigger picture, and we were stuck in this stage far too long.

I don't want you to spend twenty years in this same limbo, so in the next couple of chapters, I'll discuss some steps you can take to set your business and yourself free.

Lessons Learned

- Don't confuse the look of success with success.
- You have to stabilize your business, but don't get stuck there too long before you move forward.
- Sometimes, what you think is progress is just keeping up with the times.

8

Letting Go: The Small Business Owner's Paradox

Letting go is one of the hardest lessons for entrepreneurs to learn. But if you don't let go, you'll never release the potential of your business. My failure to let go for so many years held our company back.

Entrepreneurs are, by nature, possessive of their businesses. The business is their baby, they know more about it than anyone else, and they feel more capable to run it than anyone else. Also, they don't trust anyone else to care as much about the business. This inability to let go has led to the demise of many of the companies that go out of business each year. It could have been our undoing.

I think the mistake a lot of business owners make is that since they own the business, they're the boss, and what they say goes (see Myth #1, on page 35). The truth is, the business owner is the principal, and maybe the sole shareholder, but there's a huge difference between being the equity owner and resource manager versus knowing how to best manage and motivate people to make your business more valuable.

We have one business where my wife and I and some of our related entities and trusts are the majority shareholders. But other than providing advisory oversight, I have almost no input on how it's run because the folks who run it are much more competent than I am. Their knowledge of how to make the concept work and add value to our operations is what makes the business successful.

When you get this relationship right in your head, it will be one of the base concepts that will free both you and your company to excel. This is a critical part of the transition your small business must make—and one of its greatest paradoxes. When you first get started, you have to learn every facet of your business if you want to succeed. But to grow your business to scale, you have to find people with superior skills to fill every one of those positions as you continue to grow.

You probably think you're better at some jobs than anyone you can hire. No one else can balance the books, close a sale, or purchase inventory better than you can. And you may be right. But by hanging on to these types of tasks, you put the future of your business in jeopardy.

I remember the first vehicle auction I attended. As I bid, my heart was in my throat, and the anxiety of making a bad buy was nerve-wracking. We couldn't afford to make a mistake. But I survived and found a couple of techniques that gave me an advantage. In other words, I got pretty good at bidding, and I kept that job far too long.

When I finally turned those duties over to someone else, I attended the first several auctions with him. I advised him on how to bid successfully. Once I turned over the reins, I looked over the cars when they came in, reviewed the buyer's bid sheet, and asked why he'd bought a vehicle that had hidden damage or why he'd paid so much. Our buyer's name was Bud, so when he bought a lemon, we called it a Budmobile.

Did we sometimes pay too much or buy a car we shouldn't have? Of course we did, and it would kill me a little every time. But I couldn't focus on what we needed to do to grow the company if I remained wrapped up in every minute detail. So I had to learn to let it go.

This was actually much harder than when I let go of the tasks I didn't like to do. It was fairly easy to find someone much better than me to perform those tasks. But it's critical, even though counterintuitive, that you let someone who is not as good as you are at certain things to take on those tasks.

When you hire a new person who comes up with a plan that you've already tried, it's easy to say, "No, we're not going to do that. We tried before and it failed." The better tack is to explain what you did and why it failed. And if the new person still wants to proceed, let him, even if you're pretty sure it won't work. Let him learn from his mistakes, just like you did. This is how an organization scales its knowledge. Also, just because it didn't work when you tried it doesn't mean that he won't make a few tweaks and find a way to make it succeed.

When I first started, I had all these hats to wear, and I had to learn as much as possible about every aspect of our business. It was easy for me to take off the hats I didn't like, such as shop management, dispatch and driver management, and human resources. I knew there were people better equipped for those positions than me, plus they all reported to me. I kept a tight rein on certain things and insisted that I write and sign every check and even make all of our bank deposits.

When you're dying of thirst, you know you need water, but you may not know where to get it. Well, we were dying, and I couldn't put my finger on what was killing us. There was a clear void in my abilities and what needed to be accomplished, so I hired a controller, who, of course, reported to me. That helped but still didn't give us anywhere near the help we needed, which was to find someone else whom these managers could report to—someone with operations experience and expertise to help us grow.

I finally hired a guy as vice president and kept him busy with small projects. Every time we met, he said the same thing. "Craig, you have to let go!"

And I'd reply, "I know. I will. Just give me a little more time."

After a few months of this, I finally figured out what was wrong. The next time he said, "You have to let go," I looked him in the eye and said, "You're right, and I'm going to let you go."

You see, I didn't *trust* this guy enough to turn my business over to him. Trust is the most important factor in a marriage, and it's one of the most important factors when you choose someone to take care of your business.

Trust is the most important factor in a marriage, and it's one of the most important factors when you choose someone to take care of your business.

I wanted our business to soar, but it was starting to stall, so I continued to look for the answer. After a couple more attempts, I connected with our eventual CEO, Mike Pinckard. Mike had experience in the armored car business, where trust is crucial. But even more important, that type of business has key performance indicators (KPIs) and processes that keep everyone honest. I really couldn't afford to hire Mike, but I couldn't afford not to hire him either.

I made Mike an offer, but he received a better one from another company. Even so, we kept in touch, and when he became concerned about some of his new company's business practices, he joined our team. Since it was my second time around to fill this role, I persuaded Mike to start under the guise of a quality control position. He was trained in Six Sigma, a set of techniques and tools for process improvement. This position gave him access to every area of our business, and he could really dig into our operation to look for ways to improve our processes. The other employees were impressed with his abilities, so when he was named operations manager, no one was surprised.

I soon learned that Mike was the most moral and trustworthy leader I could have found, and his roles continued to grow. He was the perfect person to fill the voids in my abilities. Mike eventually went to Harvard Business School three weeks a year—for three years—on the company's dime. As usual, he jumped in with both feet to learn everything he could to be sure we were both getting our money's worth.

We were, and he brought tremendous value back with him through those lessons and the contacts he made. Since Mike joined the company, we've grown more than tenfold and are poised to do that again over the next few years. For the past seven years or so, only one person has reported to me: Mike. You can't imagine how good that feels!

I went from being the person who held back the company's progress because I couldn't let go, to doing the part of the business I enjoyed and had the talent to do. In other words, I spent my time working *on* the business, not *in* the business. It's a tough transition and not intuitive, but it's a journey every business owner must take to get their organization to the next level.

Years ago, guys in our CEO Vistage group would say they were worked to death and would love to be like me someday. They wanted to work on what they wanted to work on, when they wanted to work on it. I told them their problem was they had too much ability. I was terrible at management and detail-oriented work, so I had to let those duties go to someone else. These other business owners were intelligent and hard-working and talented in areas that still caused them grief.

It's hard to let go of duties that are critical to your business success if you think you can do them better than anyone else. But you have no choice. If you want your business to grow and work for you and your future, you have to let go. These guys just couldn't let go. It wasn't in their nature. It's probably not in anyone's nature. Letting go is an effort and a discipline we must adopt for the greater good of our companies.

A handful of people can micro-manage a large company and still succeed, but many more leaders get in the way of their company's success and become the single biggest impediment to reaching enterprise scale—at least $100 million a year in sales. I learned this the hard way. My LinkedIn profile summary has read the same for years: "Business owner who tries his best to get out of the way of a very talented management team."

There are a couple of lessons here. You must find a person you trust and respect enough to turn over the reins of your company. And then you have to gradually let go of all that you can. Don't expect to turn over all your duties overnight; I sure couldn't. First let go of some smaller duties that you don't like to do or those you aren't good at, and feel the burden start to lift. When you hire the best leader you can find, give him the opportunity to succeed and invest in his success. He will attract other highly talented managers and executives to take your business to the next level and beyond.

There's nothing else I've done to move the business higher than hiring the right person to lead our company. It gives you the freedom to let go of all your management or employee functions to truly grasp your role as a business owner. This is how I became a better owner with the time to envision and focus on the future of our company.

Lessons Learned

- If you want to grow, you have to let go!
- Pick your business partners with the same care you choose your spouse. The importance of trust can't be overemphasized.

9

Choose to Have a Professionally Run Business and Attract the Best Professionals

I was interested to find out what happened to a lot of mom-and-pop, or family-run, companies after they went to second or third generations because they often failed to keep things going. It often seemed like the successor's only qualification was his or her last name. I didn't want to take this chance with our business, so I decided to have our company professionally managed by the most qualified people we could find, even though we had four smart kids.

I know there are a lot of founders who want to keep their company in the family. Just make sure you do it for the right reasons and in the right way.

Even first-generation entrepreneurs often think that just because they own the business, they're more qualified than anyone else to be the boss. Business ownership and business management are two totally different jobs. As a business owner, it's your duty to find the most qualified people to fill the roles required to run your business. It only took me twenty years to figure this out! You are the principal shareholder, and it's your fiduciary responsibility to your shareholders (even if it's only you and your spouse) to hire the best talent to manage and grow that asset. The best people won't want to work for you if they think you'll replace them when your kid is ready to join the company.

You've probably seen shows on TV where someone comes in to fix a broken bar, restaurant, or hotel. Almost always, the owner had the money to get the business started but had no clue how to operate it. And the owner won't admit to having a problem but will think, "Hey, it's my money and I'm the boss." Many small businesses fail with that kind of mindset.

That attitude didn't make sense to me. It was obvious that I was a terrible manager and that I needed help. So I made the decision that, once things started to move forward, we would have the best team work for us to run the business. That's easier said than done when you're small and struggling. You have to put your business in the best possible light with promise for the future with a believable vision, and only then will the right people be attracted to you. We'll get more into that in chapter 14 on vision.

My first action was to decide to own a professionally run business, and the second action was to figure out how to sell my vision to others so they'd join our company. The third action was to figure out where we needed the most help the soonest.

It's amazing how much you don't know. We had a guy running our shop who was the best shop manager we ever had. When he was on the job, everything ran like clockwork. He could order parts without looking up the part number. He could supervise the mechanics to make sure they did the job correctly and put out a great product. He could control costs, and he was a really nice guy that people loved to work for. We thought we had filled the position with the right guy.

We had to let him go. Why? He simply wasn't scalable, and he wouldn't or couldn't change. As soon as he'd leave the building, nothing got done because there were no policies and procedures. He claimed he didn't need them, that they would only slow him down. What he didn't see was that we were a fast-growing, 24/7 operation with multiple locations, and we needed to have policies in place that allowed the shops to function around the clock, no matter who was in the lead.

This is an example of having to leave an employee behind who got you to one level of success, but was incapable of going to the next. It's one of the toughest things you have to do as an owner–either part ways with them or move them to a different position for the sake of the company.

We had a good shop manager years earlier, too. The problem was that he was also good at temper tantrums. He would throw his keys at me and say something like, "I can't deal with this guy anymore. It's either him or me."

One day, he stormed into my office, threw his keys down on the desk, and said he'd had it with so and so.

"It's either him or me," he said.

That time, I was ready for him. I already had a plan in place for the inevitable ultimatum. I thanked him for his service, picked up the keys, and wished him well. From that day forward, whenever anyone said that to me, I said, "It's definitely *you*," and the fate of the other guy would be decided later.

A few days later, he came by to get his check and clean out his office.

"I didn't think you'd take my keys," he said.

I told him that he'd obviously thought wrong and that we wouldn't let another employee run roughshod over the business by threatening to quit. I also decided that no matter how talented an employee was, if they had a toxic attitude that made the workplace unacceptable for others, they had to go regardless of the short-term pain. Life is just too short to put up with bad behavior. In the long term, we were better off.

Most employees appreciate an owner who walks the walk, is never satisfied with the size or complexity of the organization, and who isn't afraid to have an occasional risk-it-all conviction to create something new. Sadly, your organization will outgrow the abilities of many of your people (like the first shop manager I described), but that gives room to add new people with the talent and abilities to succeed at the next level.

At the same time, however, employees who aren't challenged enough will be able to show how their abilities can grow along with the company. I'm always proudest of employees who've been with us for years and have been able to grow and adapt as the company has grown and adapted. They upped their game to the level for them *and* the company to succeed together.

Your company is little more than the culture you create, the quality of the employees you hire, and how you take care of them.

Your company is little more than the culture you create, the quality of the employees you hire, and how you take care of them. A great product–no matter what it is–will never sustain success without committed, involved employees.

In our early years, we weren't a very attractive company to work for. People didn't brag that they worked for a cab company, so we often settled for folks who agreed to work for us because no one else would hire them. They had limited options, and the best and the brightest weren't beating down our door. We realized this situation wouldn't move the company where we needed to go, so we made a concerted effort to make our business more attractive to potential employees outside the cab business.

Most of our managers weren't sold on this idea because they thought the cab business was so unique that someone from the outside would find it difficult to learn what we do. But I pushed back on this because I believed that a cab company was just as unique as every other business was unique. In other words, we had a lot in common with other businesses that also had to promote themselves, manage their people and processes, and control their finances. And we didn't excel in these functions at that time. So my task was to make our business more attractive to top talent. No one wants to work in a crappy environment with a lousy culture and no prospect of growth. So it's up to us, the business owners, to make these changes.

We moved from a depressing location into a building that was so nice people would come in and ask where the cab company was! We got the building during a time of depressed rent under very favorable terms. Then we outfitted the building with artwork and office furniture from auctions at a fraction of the cost of new. Prospective employees, clients, and suppliers wanted to work with us because we looked prosperous. We were so much more efficient in our new headquarters, and that efficiency more than paid the rent.

It kind of amazed me how the appearance of prosperity was all we needed to attract better talent. Of course, that just gets people through the door. You still have to give them reasons to stay. When you are able to attract people with an idea and a vision of the future, and give them the power and environment to execute on that vision–and even permission to fail if necessary–then you unleash a rocket ship.

The right leaders attract the right people, like a magnet attracts iron filings. Other superior leaders will want to be part of that leader's team. So it's not as much about making a lot of hires to get your organization off the ground as it is to hire the type of people others will want to work for and follow.

One friend told me, "I know your secret to success."

"Oh really?" I said. "What's that?"

"You hired a great number two."

"No, I hired a great number one to replace me."

It's not the same thing.

We used another great technique when we brought new managers and leaders in from the outside. We asked them to hire their replacements as soon as they could. Hopefully, that replacement would be even better at the job than they were.

We could always tell when we had a weak manager because he or she either put off this step or hired someone weak to protect their job. The ones who "got it" brought great people into the organization. When we asked them why we'd want them to hire their replacement, they wouldn't hesitate to answer: "This is a fast-growing company, and if I don't hire a great replacement, I can't get promoted to a new position."

Bingo!

This is a rock-solid way to build a high-performing team. What happens to the ones who are afraid to hire a good replacement? We simply do that for them—and send them on their way.

When we hired our CEO, Mike, as an operations manager, he brought the idea of KPIs to the company. We've all heard the phrase "What gets measured gets managed." And what gets managed gets improved. We started to measure everything and created trailing twelve-month reports, not only for the items we knew mattered but also for others, to see what the impact was, if any. At one time, we measured over one hundred metrics just to see what tweaks we could make to move the ball.

When we hired the right people, it got us started in the right direction. But our organization still hadn't flipped the switch to a fast-growth model.

Lessons Learned

- Your company deserves the best employees that you can attract.
- Take the steps needed to make your business attractive to the best people.

10

Banks Hate You. Change That.

"A bank is a place where they lend you
an umbrella in fair weather and ask
for it back when it begins to rain."

—Robert Frost

Robert Frost had it right. It took me way too long to figure out what banks wanted to see before they would consider our business and me a good risk. There were guys who I knew were phonies who received loans I knew they couldn't repay, while I struggled to get credit, even though I was a good payer. A banker finally told me that we paid too well. When they give you a five-year loan, they want it paid off in five years, not two. I took those words to heart and borrowed only what we needed for the period of time it would take to pay it back.

Before I even got started in business, I established a relationship with the branch manager at a bank down the street from the office. I had a commission job, and she noticed I was very disciplined about saving for our (then) two kids' college education. She also took note of the increasing size of the deposits, as my income got better.

I mentioned that we had some rental properties and were thinking about buying a business.

She surprised me and said, "I think you're a good risk and the bank would be willing to establish a $25,000 credit line based on your signature alone."

We couldn't believe it. We soon took out the limit and combined it with some of our savings to buy our first business, the daycare center.

Banks hate small businesses, especially unproven, undercapitalized ones. Even if they advertise, "We love small business," they're not talking about you, the unproven, fairly new entrepreneur. They're talking about the firmly established small business that's been throwing off revenue for years. It didn't take me long to figure out that banks loan only to businesses that aren't desperate for money but need it as a tool, so they can run their business without disruption to cash flow.

There were a couple of frustrating instances. One involved that personal line of credit. Our original banker got promoted, and a new banker took her place. We would pay the line down and then tap into it to cover extra payrolls, etc. One day our new banker called to find out why the balance sometimes jumped to a higher level. I told him that it was a line of credit, and we used it when we needed to cover a third monthly payroll with the daycare center. Then we paid it down as the business could afford to.

The new banker said, "You're using this line for business? It's not for that. It's for personal use."

I said, "You mean if we blow it on a huge family trip to Hawaii, it's okay? But to use it to grow a business, so we can make more money, is taboo?"

"Yes, exactly!" he exclaimed.

Then the bank froze our line and said we could only pay it down from that day forward. I never mentioned that we'd originally used it to buy our first business.

Another time in the very early days, I wanted to borrow money to buy ten cabs.

I told the banker, "I'd like to borrow $30,000 to buy ten income-producing cabs."

He freaked out. "That's too much money to loan for such a risky investment."

I asked, "Are we a good enough risk that we could borrow the same amount to buy a Porsche for personal use?"

"Sure, your payment history supports that."

I just didn't get it. How could we qualify for loans that supported an extravagant lifestyle, but not our budding business?

So what did we do to overcome this problem? We decided that we had to establish the discipline to self-finance, so we wouldn't need banks. We had a capital-intensive business, and we had to have access to funds to grow. If the banks wouldn't loan us the cash we needed, we had to establish a corporate savings scheme.

After that, we created a vehicle leasing company and made self-imposed payments to it every month. When we needed the funds, they were available. We never slowed down. The more vehicles our leasing company leased to the cab fleet, the more money the cab fleet paid in to fund future growth. We eventually purchased hundreds of cars free and clear through the use of this savings technique. The banks appreciated our discipline and the way we grew the business.

They didn't, however, like our meager margins, but eventually gave us a $90,000 credit line to help us fund accounts receivable because much of our business had moved from cash customers to account customers. We managed that line, and every year they increased it.

Eventually, the banks would compete to loan us money. They perceived us as a good risk, but it took years to get there. Banks are on a constant lookout for customers they trust and proven small businesses that will someday be large ones. We've been very loyal to our bank through the years.

This probably sounds easier than it is, but there are many great lessons to take from this. We used to have competitors pop up, and they told everyone they were going to take over the world because they had a "money man" who was their financial backer. I always liked to hear this threat because we were using our own money–the company's money–and we couldn't afford to fail. They could fail–and almost always did.

Because we had to depend on our own funds, we religiously funded a war chest, so if an opportunity was presented that could help us grow, or if we could get a great deal, we had the funds to do it. Banks appreciate and want to work with someone who has this kind of discipline because it makes them feel good about the risk. They may start you small, but they want to grow the relationship as much as you do. You don't borrow to support a lavish lifestyle but to take advantage of ever-growing opportunities.

I can't tell you how many companies have gone out of business because they were what they described as "too successful" and couldn't afford to purchase inventory necessary to fill all their orders that, if fulfilled, would let them grow to that next level. That's not success.

You achieve success when you put your company in a position to succeed because you have all the bases covered—or at least most. (Sometimes you have to fake it until you truly make it!) I know we promised some things that we didn't actually have at that moment, but we knew we could deliver before the contract started. When you take a disciplined path to plan for the future, you consider all your needs. And you have to have the infrastructure, the leadership, the systems, and the financial wherewithal to pull it off.

We had to invest in large yards, shops, and call centers, and once we reached a certain size, it made the most sense to buy rather than lease our own facilities, so we could make them fit our specific needs.

Real estate is very tricky. It's an asset until it no longer meets your needs, and then it becomes a liability. But if purchased correctly, real estate can enhance your personal wealth as you form new entities to own these assets and then lease those premises to your operating companies.

We bought several million dollars of commercial real estate for our business operations in one year by remortgaging our home for the down payments and taking out SBA loans for the balance. We purchased one property from an out-of-state seller who just wanted it off the books. It appraised for $1,000,000 more than we paid for it on the day we closed. That resulted in a nice bump to our personal financial statement. Speaking of personal financial statements, I update them every six months to make sure we're always moving forward.

When we bought our large headquarters property, Chris and I had to sign a huge stack of papers. There were multiple lots, and we had multiple entities that the lenders wanted to guarantee the loan. We went through the huge stack and probably had to sign our names one hundred times each.

The title clerk was amazed at how fast we signed the papers. She asked, "How did you do that so fast?"

I laughed and said, "It really speeds up the process if you don't stop to read the papers."

She was flabbergasted. "You've got to be kidding!"

"Don't they basically say, 'If you don't pay the note, we'll take all your stuff?' "

"Yeah, pretty much," she admitted.

I don't mean to sound cavalier because this is serious business. I knew the value this property would add to our company, and I had little fear of failing. You have to sign a lot of large notes as a business owner, and it's fairly easy if you have a strong conviction about your ability to succeed.

We recently paid off the last bit of debt on both of our homes, and I figure we must have borrowed and repaid over $5 million on them over the last thirty years. Your house can be a piggy bank you keep coming back to until your business can stand on its own balance sheet. We probably paid about $16,000 a month on average toward our house payment, even though our actual payment at the time was much less. Again, this discipline meant that we always had equity to turn to–on our own terms–whenever we needed it.

We did get on the outs with our bank several years ago when they changed our business classification. When we were considered a small business, we did $10 million to $20 million a year in sales and maybe had a $1 million line of credit. We were something of a big fish in that category. Based on our growth and trajectory, they decided to reclassify us as a midsize business. A midsize business was defined as one that grossed $20 million to $200 million. We were just barely at $20 million at that time.

The bank assigned us a new representative, and apparently we weren't worth his time. He kept dropping the ball on our account. We finally had enough, and I called the bank to tell them that we were thinking about moving our account to another bank. I'd been with them personally for twenty-five years and had a business relationship for twenty, and we felt like they took us for granted, as evidenced by their poor service. They met with us and introduced us to a new team, and they couldn't have been more sincere and apologetic. The shoe was on the other foot, and they didn't want to risk losing a really good customer.

The senior bank leader asked me, "What do you want? How can we keep you as a customer?"

"I'm very disappointed because I've been a loyal customer all these years," I said. "I want to have the same relationship with your large bank that my dad had with his small town bank. Dad would sit across the banker's desk and tell him his company's needs. The banker would agree to the amount and terms, and they would shake hands on the deal and be done."

The banker looked at me and said, "That's it? I don't see why we can't do that."

The new team was wonderful to work with, and they increased our borrowing ability every year.

A couple of years later, we had our annual meeting with the bank. They brought in their team, the CEO, and their highest-ranked credit advisor in the state. Our CFO had shared our financials and his ideas about our needs with the bank before we met.

In the meeting, our CFO stood up and gave a small presentation. He told the bankers what our needs would be for the coming year.

The credit advisor came over, shook my hand, and said, "You got it!"

"You mean the amount and terms we requested?"

"Yes," he replied. "I've done this on a handshake only one other time, and it was with you and your team last year. It's rare that we get a chance to do this, but you and your team have proven that you do what you say you'll do, and we trust you. You are growing your company at a fantastic rate when many of our customers are shrinking or simply not growing at all."

Our diligence had paid off, and we finally got our banking relationship on par, or even better than, my dad had experienced.

Several years ago, our bankers came to our corporate holiday party and pulled Chris and me aside to ask for a quick meeting before the party started. I looked at her and thought, *Now what*?

We went down the hall to my office, and they pulled our personal guarantees for all of our loans from a thick folder. Then they handed us a giant pair of scissors to cut them up. The guarantees were no longer necessary, they said, as our businesses now stood on their own.

I finally felt like we had really made the transition from a homegrown company to a formal corporate entity.

When you use your own money, it's a good gauge to find out if your business is sustainable. Businesses either have to make money or have a clear path to how they will make money in the near future. Years ago, I listened to a spiel about a C-store gas station chain that was looking for franchisees. After the guy laid out the numbers, he asked, "Well, what do you think?"

I said, "I think I want to be you because I can't see any money in this for the franchisee."

Several years later, I was at the bank and met two brothers who were there. They told me they operated three of those same C-stores as franchisees.

I said, "Man, I don't know how you pay your bills and all the fees, and still pay for the franchise."

"We don't," they said, "We couldn't afford that. Our father bought the franchise for us because there wasn't enough profit in the deal to pay back the franchise fee."

A couple of years later, they lost all three stores. If they had been forced to use their own money, they either would have never done the deal or would have seen the handwriting on the wall and gotten out before they lost everything.

Early on, we created a path that allowed us to reach success across the board by putting the odds in our favor. We did it by building up cash through the job I hated but that paid me well—the auditing job I quit when I was thirty.

I tell my kids if you're going to work at a job, do something you love, something for the experience, or something for the money, so you can do what you want. If you're lucky, it's more than one of the above.

Our approach may sound super conservative, but don't get me wrong. We love using other people's money to fund our operations. At our size, we'd be lost without it. We just always keep in mind that whatever we borrow isn't ours. It's someone else's money, and it has to be repaid.

We treat money as a tool, and a very powerful one. Good debt funds your growth at an exponential rate. Bad debt to support your lifestyle can be devastating.

As your company continues to grow, you must match your head of finance position to the complexity of your needs. Smaller companies may want to outsource this function until the need is too great. Then you'll want a controller to work with your banks and oversee accounting. You may need some CFO advice, and you can get away with outsourcing that function as well, until you need an in-house CFO.

Your CFO will help negotiate with the banks and bring his or her existing relationships to your company. A great CFO will pore over contracts to make sure all the terms are in your best interest. And when the time comes for mergers and acquisitions, the new CFO will help lead your company through those processes.

I recommend that you don't hire too much more than you need at the time. Finance guys like situations that stretch their abilities. If you overhire, you'll probably get a guy who gets bored quickly and starts to look for a more challenging position with another firm.

This is true with all your lead positions. You want to hire folks who have more ability than you currently need but not so much that they don't have a path to the job they eventually want to do. If you hire a couple of levels up, you'll pay a lot of money for a bad fit for your organization.

Lessons Learned

- It's never too early to establish a relationship with a bank.
- Your word matters. Don't ever overpromise and then underdeliver.
- When you use your own money, you have no choice but to succeed. You can't afford to fail.
- Oversize your improvements so you have room to grow.
- Don't overlook any equity you have. Your house can be a terrific piggybank.
- If you do a good job taking care of the bank, they won't want to lose you as a customer. Take advantage of being in the driver's seat.
- Don't confuse what your growing company makes with what you should be paid.

11

Flipping the Rapid-Growth Switch

By now you've figured out that we transitioned from a small cab company to a major player in the personal transportation and technology business that generates hundreds of millions of dollars a year through our various divisions. After being stuck for so many years, what finally changed?

> We transitioned from a small cab company to a major player in the personal transportation and technology business.

I got a second chance in the cab business and was determined not to fail. But I didn't have a passion for *that* business. I wasn't what anyone would consider a cab guy. I figured we'd build it up and then sell it and get a real business. Then something changed.

It didn't happen overnight, but it didn't take long to transform my mindset and the mindset of the company. A couple of things served as the catalyst.

The first was the change in our organization after Mike took over as president. I always had plenty of ideas but really stunk at execution.

In the early nineties, Super Shuttle had captured a lot of the long runs to the airport. Super Shuttle is an airport shuttle service that people use most often when traveling alone because the taxi fare would be excessive. However, they might have three stops on the way to the airport, so travelers have to leave at least three hours before their flights. My idea was to start Discount Shuttle and guarantee that there would be no more than one extra stop on the way to the airport.

We registered the name, we ran ads in the Yellow Pages, and we obtained phone lines. But I never completed the plan by setting up flat rates to the airport. We captured some extra work, but my lack of follow-through prevented the plan from really succeeding.

After Mike came on board, I would discuss an idea with him, and he would try to tear it apart. It seemed like he always had more questions than I had answers. Mike has the annoying, but effective, habit of always answering a question with a question of his own.

When his people ask a question, he always says something like, "I don't know. What do you think?" Then after they tell him what they think, he digs further by asking what brought them to that conclusion. Sometimes, he prevented the company from going down a rabbit hole; but other times, he'd figure out how to accomplish the new task and put all the pieces in place to make it happen. We actually executed the plan and transformed our visions into reality.

We bid on a large airport contract and won, which forced a former competitor to sell their business. At that point, we became the second-largest cab company in our market. The change in our organization was amazing, and our successes made me feel much different about our business. I still wasn't a fan of the cab business, but we were making progress, and the impact we could make definitely resonated with me.

Some people think they're following their passion, but they've really only turned their favorite hobby into a business—which they hated. I went into a fly shop in Phoenix one time and talked to the owner. He had a true passion for fly-fishing and had a wonderful shop. I asked him about some of the lines he carried, and he was very helpful.

Then I asked, "So what are some of your favorite places to fish, and how are they fishing right now?"

He looked up at me from the counter and frowned. He said, "Well, I used to like this creek or that river, but I haven't been in so long that I can't tell you how they're fishing."

He said that his fly shop in the middle of the desert required him to be there all day, six days a week, and he had to get all his chores done on his day off. You see, he loved everything about fly-fishing, but he didn't love the business that actually kept him away from doing what he loved.

A couple of years later, I went by his shop, but he was no longer in business. I hope he found his way back to the streams and his passion.

Once we saw we could do anything we set out to do, we doubled down and put our money where our mouth was. We went on a tear to invest in the infrastructure needed to support our goals. One of the earliest goals was to build one of the top five taxi companies in the United States. To do this, we had to expand our locations.

We moved from our nice main facility on two acres to an even nicer new facility on twelve acres.

We opened up the East Valley office on five acres and a new facility in Tucson on four acres. This physical expansion allowed us to grow into public transportation, operate and repair buses, and maintain the huge shops needed to keep our fleets on the road. The larger new facilities meant we could grow our taxi fleet from around three hundred vehicles to almost twelve hundred, and we still have room to grow. Our transit authority would never have even considered letting us operate buses if we didn't have such expansive facilities. When you have an asset-heavy business, you can't grow if you don't have space to accommodate that growth.

We moved and expanded our dispatch center three times at our headquarters before we built a custom remodeled building with full UPS and generator backup, which allows us to operate around the clock and support other markets. We eventually co-located our IT systems and then moved all of our servers and systems to the cloud. We went from twenty operator desks to seventy-five, to one hundred twenty-five to an unlimited number with call takers who can work from home. Now we can grow our call center unabated, and our facilities don't limit our growth as we add new accounts and new service areas.

We wrote our own software and systems to create a competitive advantage because we felt constrained by the off-the-shelf software that most companies used. We eventually had as many as twenty people on our IT staff.

We established a policy of continuous improvement that meant we never settled for what we had. We made a point to always get facilities, infrastructure, and people that gave the company room to grow to the next level. By the way, the next level continues to evolve with the growth of your business. It never stops!

Sometimes the progress seemed slow and was hard to see. At other times, such as when we moved to a new facility, purchased a new computer platform, or started a new division, the change was dramatic. The point is that you never stop moving your business forward.

We moved to facilities that our existing business could barely support, we hired people who had the track record to get our business to the next level, and as the owner, I did everything in my power to make everyone involved successful. Then I got out of their way so they could bring that success to the whole enterprise. We made these moves to put the odds in our favor because success attracts better employees and better customers.

At one of our strategy sessions, I laid out an ambitious plan to our management. In it, our company was envisioned as the solution not just locally, but nationally.

After the meeting, Mike pulled me aside and asked, "Are you sure that's the direction you want to go? You have a pretty nice lifestyle and profitable company now."

"Yes," I replied. "I really believe in our mission and our team's ability to get things done. I want to push toward this vision."

Again Mike pressed me. "Are you sure? You get to go home every night and be with your family. Going this direction will require a lot of travel to oversee that many locations."

"Mike, I know the travel has to be done, but I'm not the one who's going to do it."

I had now accepted my role as the owner, not a manager, and it gave me the freedom to dream big. Mike went to work to make the vision a reality.

We had a target to grow around 50 percent a year, and we actually grew an average of 40 percent a year from 2008 to 2016. Now, we were disappointed if we didn't hit our BHAG (big hairy audacious goal), but I think we're still in the ballpark. Most people would kill for that kind of growth.

Here's what Mike believes was responsible for our phenomenal growth:

1. **Our vision is supported by specific sales goals.**

   We always put numbers to our goals. We looked at any opportunities coming up in the next twelve months and asked the managers what they needed to take advantage of these opportunities and achieve these goals.

   Things never go as you plan, but if everyone in the company knows that the company has an expectation to hit a certain sales goal—and different divisions and areas also have their own goals—they pull out all the stops to achieve those goals. If we lost one of our expected opportunities, we asked that team what the revised plan was to hit their goal. Not hitting the goal wasn't an option. Our managers thrived under this expectation. We created a take-no-prisoners and make-no-excuses environment.

   A great example of this was the time we lost the airport bid. We had the contract for the two previous contract periods, but the airport decided to open up it up to the highest bidder, not the most qualified. We bid an amount that made us nervous, but our competitor agreed to pay over

$16,000 per cab per year for a contract for which we'd paid only $300 per cab per year. They "won" the bid but got hit so hard financially that they couldn't support their account and call-in work.

We lost sixty-five airport cabs that we probably would have operated at a loss had we won the contract. But we replaced them in less than three months with over one hundred street cabs that generated full leases with no payouts. We never missed a beat, and we exceeded the budget in cab leases and income for the year. We also became the largest cab company in town.

2. **We built our organizational design and structure to achieve those goals.**

The most important issue here was when we moved away from a cost-center structure and built a true profit-based, general-management structure. We originally had site managers who were responsible to manage operating costs for their specific areas in a decentralized structure, while sales and pricing were centralized under the control of a completely separate sales organization. This structure ultimately disconnected revenue generation from operating cost control, and no one was responsible for profitability. As a result, decisions that drove down operating costs would often drive down revenue by more than was saved, or revenues were added at levels below our operating-cost levels.

A great example of this was with our Meditrans division. This division provides full-size wheelchair lift vans with hourly employees. We offered a terrific service that was very expensive to provide and that no one could afford. The Meditrans manager was supposed to price, grow, and manage his business, but his performance measures had no accountability to profits. As a result, he was successful at growing the business by effectively "selling dollars for 99 cents." The more he grew the business, the more money we lost. When we aligned accountability for revenues, costs, and profits under the general manager's responsibilities, our growth and profitability began to soar.

We had to make sure that our infrastructure and fleet investments would support our goals, and another example of this was when we added functional support to our organizational design through a matrix-type management structure. This structure gave our general managers the technical support needed to run their businesses but also respected their decision-making autonomy. This structure discouraged the natural inclination to create silos and mini-fiefdoms that are present in most organizations.

3. **We established a clearly defined strategy to achieve sales success.**

   Our sales organization was fully integrated into our organizational structure with full accountability to our general managers.

   Technical sales support and direction was provided through a matrix relationship between the general managers and the director of business development. Each general manager was charged to work with his sales team and our corporate support staff to build the sales strategy best suited to their specific markets.

4. **We started to measure the things that really matter.**

Probably one of our most important KPIs was "trips per lease day," which allowed us to ensure that passenger satisfaction, driver success, and financial performance were all properly aligned. Many times employees are fooled by false information that is created when two incomparable periods are compared. By taking into account the number of days in a month and any holidays, we made it clear to our managers that we had to maintain a certain ratio to ensure everyone's success. So they focused like laser beams on growing the business in a way that properly managed this crucial relationship. Service levels improved, which increased demand, and driver earnings improved, which further improved service. This created a kind of self-fulfilling prophecy that allowed us to grow at a phenomenal rate for years.

A former sales manager used to ring a bell every time one of his sales guys got a signed contract. But while a signed contract might seem like an appropriate measure, those contracts didn't require the customer to use our services. As a result, the sales people were earning commissions for getting contracts signed, even though those signed contracts, taken by themselves, did nothing to increase revenues. We got paid for transporting passengers, not for signed contracts.

When we changed our sales measurement to actual trips performed, we aligned sales activity with our desired outcomes, and trip volumes and revenues dramatically increased.

We tried to take all the chatter out of our results. For instance, we measured lease days per accident so we could see if an increase in accident frequency reflected greater carelessness or if the rate of incidences had actually gone down from the prior period. We focused on the right leading indicators rather than lagging indicators because we wanted to be clear about where we were going and what measures would take us there, not where we had been.

5. **We implemented variable compensation.**

We want to reward people when they achieve specific sales goals. At the same time, if a division fails to hit their goals, it affects everyone's compensation throughout the company. On the other hand, if someone exceeds expectations, it improves not only their compensation, but also their teammates' compensation. This encouraged our managers to collaborate with each other and share best practices.

We believed in our core that when variable compensation is implemented correctly, it should self-fund, should properly share value between employees and the company, and most importantly, should reward employees for creating the desired financial results. As such, we believed that capping variable compensation violates the principle of properly sharing value because it shifts the value created by employees disproportionately to the company.

You remember my earlier disgust when my commissions were throttled in my old auditing position? That's why this became a crucial tenant of mine. We believed that variable compensation created a true win-win-win relationship for our customers, employees, and the company. This is the premise for all of our programs.

Once we implemented these programs throughout our company, our growth and profitability accelerated and employee earnings increased dramatically. Now we could attract and retain better and better people. It created a mechanism for continuous improvement.

Case in point: We had a business development associate who was several rungs down the ladder from our C-suite leaders. One year, he slayed a giant account at a good margin, and as a result made more money that year than his managers and most of the C-suite. But nobody complained because they had all benefited from the sale and the margins it created. A rising tide lifted all boats, as it should.

6. **We aligned management accountability and responsibility to ensure appropriate focus.**

In many companies, the departments set goals for sales and other achievements, but they fail to give their employees the autonomy and control necessary to achieve those goals. In a larger company like ours with hundreds of employees and thousands of independent contractors in multiple markets, it's imperative that accountability and responsibility are properly aligned.

A good example of misalignment reared its ugly head early on in our development. One of our major obstacles to growth was our inability to effectively manage the relationship between demand for services (trips) and the supply (drivers and vehicles) needed to meet that demand. At the time, these two critical elements were managed independently of each other.

Our sales department was responsible for creating demand, while the operations department was responsible for providing the supply. This created never-ending finger-pointing between sales and operations. Sales complained that there were never enough vehicles to service their customers, and operations argued that sales wasn't providing enough trips to support additional vehicles. While our organizational structure made our general managers responsible for managing this relationship, the traditional separation of duties was dramatically jeopardizing our growth.

To resolve this conflict and properly align responsibilities, we shifted responsibility for both supply and demand to our sales organization and defined key metrics around managing the supply-and-demand relationship. This simple, but crucial, change unleashed our company's potential and was more responsible for improving our sales and revenue growth than any other single change we made.

You can't hand your team a gun and a target but no bullets.

When employees believe they're in complete control over their job responsibilities, it fundamentally changes their level of ownership and commitment to the cause. Your people want to be challenged and given the tools to succeed. You can't hand your team a gun and a target but no bullets. This pride shows through and is their reason to get out of bed every morning because it's more than just a job.

We weren't perfect at this with 100 percent of our employees, but we worked very hard to align responsibility and true control, and we believe it had a lot to do with the evolution of our culture.

7. **We created regular reports displaying results, and adopted regular meetings to review performance and adjust action plans.**

   We wouldn't just "set it and forget it" with our goals. We created reports, some daily and some less frequent, to give us real-time information on our progress. If we find that one area isn't hitting its expectations, we create an action plan to get them back on track. These findings and reviews help keep our whole organization on the right path.

8. **We created a culture where sales growth is expected.**

   Nothing succeeds like success. Once you set outsized goals and achieve them, the whole organization develops a can-do attitude. We believed we were better than any other company, and we believed we could achieve anything. That's a fun place to be as an organization and an owner.

Applying these disciplines to your own company can move it from its current state to a new and exciting future. It starts with seeing your business as what you imagine it can be and then working toward that vision.

Lessons Learned

- Discover your passion and apply it to your business's purpose.
- Don't confuse doing what you love with running a business in that same field if business isn't your passion.
- Find the disciplines outlined in this chapter and determine how to apply them to your company.

12

Take Care of Your Most Important Asset

It doesn't matter how good your product and systems are if you don't have engaged employees. The larger you grow, the truer this becomes. When your people interact with your customers, they reflect your company values and show how important those customers are to your organization.

We have thousands of customer touch points in our organization, and it was critical to get this piece of the puzzle right. At first, I put myself in charge to make sure that we took care of the soft side of taking care of our people; and Mike and our organizational folks made sure we had the right metrics to attract and retain the best people.

Maybe it was my memories of being abused as an independent contractor at the freight bill auditing company that made me want to be a fair employer and to see the workplace through employees' eyes. This gets harder as you go along because it's easy to accept the current conditions as normal.

Our working conditions were terrible in the early days. I wasn't proud of those conditions, and neither were our employees. We always made sure that each move put us into nicer offices and shops.

Today, we have offices in which we've invested millions of dollars to construct or remodel. We take the time to add interesting features and decor. Our offices are not bland or cookie cutter. In fact, we have a collection of taxicab and transportation memorabilia and artwork on display.

We commission artists for works that highlight our company and people. We encourage our people to personalize their workspaces, and we think most employees appreciate this. They spend many hours a week on the job, and we want it to be as pleasant as possible. Visitors often rave about how nice and professional our people are. We think their environment, as well as how they're treated, has a lot to do with this.

In the early days, money was tight, and we listened intently to our employees and the struggles they encountered. We often had dinner brought in on the first of the month to feed our people who were still busy on the phones. We paid our employees every other Friday, and we also had dinner brought in on the first off-payroll Friday of the month. Most of employees were pretty broke after paying their rent for the month, so they really appreciated having dinner delivered on their "broke" Friday.

After observing their responses to that, we implemented other employee-friendly policies that are still in place today. Our Christmas bonuses are strictly based on tenure. A new employee might get only $100, but it really starts to add up for the senior employees. We pay the bonuses on the last off-payroll Friday before Christmas, so it's like an extra payday. I can't tell you how often our people tell us that this makes their Christmas possible.

We also have a catered Christmas party right on the premises so that even employees who have to work a shift can share in the fun. We hold it in the shop where we all have room to sit together. We're a 24/7 operation, so we always have people on duty, although the mechanics always close the shop early for the day to enjoy the Christmas party.

To make it even more festive, we give our Excellence in Motion team a budget, and they go to several big-box retailers to buy stacks of gifts to raffle off. Almost everyone wins something, and we always give away a nice grand prize. Those parties are a great time to talk and break bread with the troops. And they give us a chance to have different departments meet each other and for the leadership to mix with employees other than those they normally work with.

The Excellence in Motion Committee was founded over fifteen years ago, and it has volunteer representatives from most departments. The committee is involved in several activities. The members choose an Employee of the Month from nominations from the various managers. Winners receive a certificate, a gift card, and a plaque with their name that's displayed in the lobby for all to see. In addition, our Total Transit Foundation donates $500 in the winner's name to the non-profit of his or her choice.

The committee also plans employee recognition events, like the annual picnic that's often held at a small amusement park. Every quarter, at a New Employee Breakfast, employees who joined us during the previous ninety days meet with me and other company leaders to get acquainted and to introduce the newbies to the culture at Total Transit.

The committee also organizes the Christmas party and the annual Employee of the Month luncheon, where the C-level executives have lunch with the previous year's winners and the members of the committee. We take advantage of these lunches to shower our Employee of the Month winners with love and affection. We let them know just how much their efforts and field leadership mean to us and our organization.

Several years ago, we looked for a program that all of our employees could access online. This program, which we dubbed The Total Transit Way, became a way for employees to recognize the above-and-beyond efforts of their peers, managers, direct reports, or anyone else they interacted with in our organization. Today, the updates are sent out weekly, and anyone in the company can add comments about the nominees. It becomes a real praise-fest, where everyone has the ability to let the nominees know how much their efforts are appreciated.

It seems like many organizations interact with their employees only when there's a problem, and we want to be different. That's why we love our program. It's all positive feedback, and this system creates the candidates for our Employee of the Month nominations.

We do other small things that mean a lot to our people. We send out cards to our employees on the anniversary of their hiring date. I usually research these employees through The Total Transit Way program so I can thank them for their specific achievements during the past year and for their service. I also send a card on every employee's birthday with a couple of movie tickets and a congratulatory note.

We go the extra step to have these cards custom-designed each year, and many employees save the series. My favorite anniversary card was a copy of a painting of a couple of employees going about their jobs with smiles on their faces. The original hangs in one of our lobbies.

A few years ago, we decided we wanted to do more for employees who had stuck with us over the years. Donna, our organizational development executive, created a recognition program that awards employees a trip to an Arizona resort at the ten-year level and trips to a regional resort for fifteen and twenty years of service, along with travel cash to cover the other expenses. We present all of this to them in a custom container constructed out of old taxicab license plates.

Many of our jobs are sedentary, and to address challenges of our employees' health, we started several initiatives. We began by offering a weight-loss challenge every year. The employee who loses the highest percentage of his or her starting weight is the winner. These challenges always get the competitive juices flowing for bragging rights, and to make sure employees stick to the plan, we have another weigh-in six months after the contest ends and give a cash reward to the employee who has kept the most weight off. We also built and equipped a very nice fitness center at our headquarters with cardio and resistance gear.

In 2013, we stepped up our efforts even more by offering a program we call Total Wellness. We hired a wellness coordinator and selected Wellness Champions in each department to help achieve our objectives. We offer free wellness tests for all our employees and have quarterly themes and guest speakers on many holistic subjects. We host a farmer's market in the offices to expose our employees to healthier choices, and we offer food preparation seminars. We offer healthier options in our vending machines, which have been very popular, and we've received awards for being a healthy place to work.

It may sound obvious, but your employees are people, not machines. I say this because I've heard of employers who don't allow their employees time off to take care of personal matters. We've had older, valued employees suffer a stroke or get into a serious medical condition that required them to take an extended amount of time off. We kept them on the payroll and encouraged them to come back to work on their own terms to do whatever they could. These employees appreciated our approach, and instead of sitting at home, they looked forward to getting better and being productive again.

So how does your organization attract the superstar employees and leaders you need to grow into a successful enterprise? You have to give them the vision and be believable. If we had settled on just being the best cab company in town, would we have attracted our talent? No. It was the vision we painted and the steps we took along the way to move toward that vision that got our people excited. They worked to create something special, something that didn't exist before, something that got them out of bed in the morning, ready to take on the next challenge. You have the vision, but your people are the ones who bring it to fruition and deliver day in and day out.

Lessons Learned

- Your employees are the most important part of your company, and they can make or break you. Attract the best and take care of them. Try to see the workplace through their eyes.

- Celebrate your employees' successes and make sure they know how important they are to you.
- A healthy employee makes for a productive workplace.
- Give your employees a vision they can believe in and help bring to fulfillment.

13

Create a Values-Based Business

What do you stand for? What do you want your business to stand for? These are your values, and there's every reason to build your company around those values. Your values fuel your purpose and make it easier to manage a growing business. It's too bad we didn't realize this sooner.

We were in business for almost twenty years before we had our first strategic planning session. Perhaps we weren't ready for that in the first few years, but we sure wasted a lot of time and probably missed plenty of opportunities to start our rapid-growth trajectory. When we started to hold strategic planning meetings, one of the first things we did was discuss our core principles, and then we put what we believed in writing. As we did this, our values revealed themselves.

Oftentimes, the binders that hold a company's strategic plans gather dust on a shelf until the next year's planning session, untouched and forgotten. So it wasn't surprising that some people considered strategic planning a waste of time and a distraction. Of course, the same things are said about annual budgets. Both work only if done correctly and if follow-up and action items are completed.

I'd just joined the CEO network, Vistage, and had listened to several speakers talk about the importance of strategic planning. After twenty years, our company was showing signs of stagnation, and we all knew we couldn't get where we needed to go without a plan. We finally decided to have our first strategic planning session in the fall of 2003, and we brought in my Vistage chair as the facilitator. The decision to bring in an outside party helped us break through the hierarchy of our respective positions. It allowed us to think like a team and develop one voice. The participants didn't wait to see what my opinion was before offering theirs, which I loved.

We had a few new higher-caliber executives who'd been through the process at their former companies. We decided to include only the C-level executives and department heads and held several small meetings before the retreat to figure out what we wanted to achieve and what we wanted to avoid during that time.

Our first session was pretty basic, and we decided it was important to embrace the basics–kind of like Vince Lombardi did in the first practice every year for the Green Bay Packers when he held a pigskin in his right hand and declared, "Gentlemen, this is a football."

We did a SWOT analysis to identify our strengths, weaknesses, opportunities, and threats. Since this was our first meeting, we didn't have a baseline against which to compare our findings, so this SWOT analysis became our baseline. Everyone likes to point out their strengths and discuss their opportunities, but most hesitate to list weaknesses and threats. When you perform a thorough deep-dive in all four areas, this drill really points out the best direction to go each year.

At first, some of our suggestions sounded downright dopey, but you can't get to the good ideas unless you throw a few flyers in there. Sometimes we dismissed a suggestion and then returned to it later with a different slant. Then we determined the people or teams to work on each area of concern, and these steps created action items and an agenda for our first quarterly review meeting.

These lists turned thoughts into actions. For example, prior to this we had informally talked about contracting with a lobbyist to protect our interests, but we never did it because we had no action plan to execute. After that meeting, a team was set up to find someone to represent our interests as our lobbyist.

There was a big problem at the time with unlicensed and uninsured taxis in Arizona. If unchecked, we were afraid it would put public safety at risk and ruin the reputation of our business. Through the efforts of our lobbyist, we got a bill passed and signed by the governor.

Before we started planning, we had a lot of great ideas. But without action, those ideas remained idle dreams. Once our teams were all rowing in the same direction and synchronized, we couldn't help but grow our company. We spent a lot of time vetting opportunities to grow as well as ways to be more efficient and reduce expenses.

We vowed not to create silos. Many companies have separate accounting departments and sales organizations that have different goals than the operational departments. I once worked for a company where the accounting department questioned every decision I made. There was no partnership. We created a variation of matrix management that had separate departments, but its members were there to support our operational department goals. This—along with the support the managers gave each other to ensure that everyone achieved their goals and maximum profit-sharing—caused the departments to support each other for the combined success of the company.

We tore into our weaknesses; we didn't seek to cast blame but to identify ideas that would reduce or eliminate our weaknesses and, where possible, turn them into strengths. Some items never got attention and probably didn't deserve any, but we gained a greater sense of clarity about what was important to the company and what changes to undertake.

The result of our strategic planning meetings was our company vision, our mission statement, our core principles, and a template for how to get to where we needed to be in one year, three years, and six years.

Our mission statement lets everyone who works for us, and that we work for, know the reason we're in business:

> **Total Transit is dedicated to providing transportation services and solutions that create customers for life and enhance the communities we serve.**

I know that's not mind-blowing. But it lets everyone know that the reason we're in business is to enhance the communities we serve, while providing innovative solutions at a level that creates customers for life. The communities we serve will be better off because we're in business to serve them, and we won't do business the way it's always been done. We will innovate to provide the best service solutions for the best rates, and we won't be satisfied with anything less. Our mission statement lets all our employees know they're expected to do more than a job. They're making our world a better place through their actions.

Early in my career, I worked for a guy who was a micromanager. He had a tremendous capacity to oversee every minute detail. Most people don't want to try to keep up on every detail. I'm certainly not wired that way. I'd rather look at the big picture. Also, micromanaging belittles the abilities and judgment of your people. We'd rather have our employees focus on doing the right thing, and that's why we formed our core principles.

I'm not sure we'd even heard the term *values-based business* before we created our core principles. Core values, or principles as we called them, are what we believe is essential to our business. Here the six core principles that are essential to our operation and our company culture:

- Manage risk and our impact on the environment
- Attract, mentor, and retain the best people
- Understand the customer's needs and exceed their expectations
- Be an indispensable member of our community
- Encourage innovation and embrace change
- Operate transparently, with honesty and integrity at all times

Core principle #1–Manage risk and our impact on the environment

In an earlier chapter, I said that our company was in "insurance hell" because we didn't know how to manage risk. When you have hundreds, then thousands of vehicles on the streets, twenty-four hours a day, 365 days a year, you have to make safety a priority. We felt that we owed it to the public, as well as our customers, to have the safest drivers on the road that we could get. We did complete background checks and created a drug-free workplace. We did this not because we had a mandate from some government agency, but because our core principles told the world that this is who we are.

We later expanded on this value when we started operating our hybrid fleet and installed four hundred solar panels at our headquarters. Reducing our negative impact on the environment is important to the way we operate.

Core principle #2–Attract, mentor, and retain the best people

Early on, this was one of the most difficult values to implement. In the early days, we weren't a very attractive company. But after several years, we no longer referred to ourselves as a cab company because we had transformed into so much more than that.

Even though we operated beautiful facilities and nurtured a good work environment, more than one prospective management employee pulled into the lot, saw what looked like a cab company, and never even got out of their vehicle. We used to say that we had the best people in any transportation company, and we did. But that wasn't enough. We had to compete against every company in every industry for the best talent, and we needed people from outside our industry for the critical skills.

We invested in recruitment tools and tests to make sure we profiled for the right people, and we kept improving our value equation so really good prospects would see us as a valuable place to work that had a future. We weren't perfect, but we got better at being slow to hire and quick to fire.

Once, when we needed to fill a general manager position, we called back a very qualified applicant, a former senior manager with UPS, for six interviews before we hired him. He later said that if we hadn't made an offer that sixth time, he probably wouldn't have come in for a seventh interview. Luckily for us, the sixth time was a charm, and he's been one of the most valuable employees in our operation for the past twelve years.

Core principle #3—Understand the customers' needs and exceed their expectations

We never wanted to overrepresent our abilities. We told customers what we could do for them, but they'd heard those promises from others before. We enjoyed the love-fest meetings we had with new customers after we started servicing their accounts and they saw that we did what we said we'd do. They were often incredulous that we could deliver on our promises because they'd been disappointed so many times in the past. That's how you create customers for life.

Core principle #4—Be an indispensable member of our community

This principle led to our eventual creation of the Total Transit Foundation in 2009. We felt we owed a debt to the communities we served because our success depended on their support. We had an informal policy of giving, but the foundation gave us the funding mechanism to push our giving to the next level. We started by contributing 6 percent of our profits to the foundation. We found that our people didn't care as much about how much money the company made. They were way more interested in how much we gave back and supported their personal giving.

We also decided that every member of our leadership team would join a non-profit board and join leadership committees to represent our company in the community. We had leaders who weren't sure if they had the time to get involved and give back, but soon these same people declared it was their favorite part of the job. It truly makes you feel good and fulfilled to help others.

For instance, we're frequently the primary sponsor for a Habitat for Humanity house, and our team gets together on weekends to help with construction. These are good projects in so many ways. Employees get to meet people from other departments, and they also see that the company lives up to our commitment to enhance the communities we serve.

As a result of these efforts, we were recently honored as one of the top large philanthropic companies in Arizona.

Core principle #5—Encourage innovation and embrace change

Innovation became more and more important as we tried to differentiate ourselves from the competition. We made huge investments in technology and infrastructure in order to stay ahead of the curve and even wrote our own software because we couldn't find a workable solution. Our IT department had fifteen to twenty employees when most of our counterparts didn't even have one full-time, dedicated IT employee.

But in the early years, we had a group of people who hated change. That's why we let everyone know up front that, not only would we change when we had to, but disruption and proactive change would always be a part of life at Total Transit. Employees would have to change or move on.

Even today, we constantly look for ways to create new systems and products to keep us relevant in the marketplace. It was almost comical during our annual reviews at the strategic planning meeting. We started off by reviewing our successes from the previous year: the new records set, record revenues, lower complaints, and better on-time service. Then we jumped right into what we could do differently in the current year to make us better. We never rested on our previous accomplishments.

Core principle #6—Operate transparently, with honesty and integrity at all times

Believe it or not, we left this last value out the first time we worked on our core principles. As we started our strategic planning session the second year, I said, "I think we missed something."

Everyone agreed, and it's probably the most important value in our company. We do what we say we're going to do and don't try to hide our actions. That means we won't say something behind someone's back that we wouldn't say to his or her face. Also, our data is an open book for our customers, and they can check our on-time performance anytime.

Everyone in our organization has to act with complete honesty, or they're out. We make this abundantly clear and have had to say goodbye to several talented people who couldn't abide by this value. That sounds rough, but if your people can't stand up to your values, they'll eventually fail and cause your company to fail in its mission. Also, your people will see that the organization really means what it says when a valuable employee is let go because of an ethics violation.

When you walk into almost every office in one of our facilities, you'll see our core principles and our mission statement proudly and prominently displayed. Does that make a difference? You're damn right it does! These posters tell everyone who works for us and everyone who visits our offices that this is who we are, this is what we do, and this is why we do it.

These posters tell everyone who works for us and everyone who visits our offices that this is who we are, this is what we do, and this is why we do it.

We even quiz our people on our principles to make sure they know them and use them in their decision-making.

Before we adopted our core principles, our employees used to ask what to do in certain situations with our customers. Or if they didn't know what to do, they referred the problem to their supervisor, who might bump the problem up to a manager. When your customer has a problem, it needs to be resolved *now*. Deferring a problem can create horrible customer service when an immediate decision is needed in a 24/7 environment. It also makes your organization appear to be disorganized and inefficient, which it is.

After the core principles were displayed throughout our facilities, we told our employees that as long as their decisions supported those core principles, they couldn't go wrong. In a values-based organization, your values make the decisions for you, and they simplify your operations as you scale.

As your business scales, and you add more and more employees who interact with your customers, following the core values empowers the employee to make a decision on the spot. A few decisions may cost the company money but, overall, these mistakes in judgment far outweigh the benefit that comes from trusted, empowered employees. And good, timely customer service yields results that are the exact opposite of what happens when employees are micromanaged. And that's a very good thing!

Lessons Learned

- Active strategic planning creates a roadmap to success.
- Once you identify what the core values are for your business and affirm their importance to your employees' actions, life becomes easier for managers, employees, and customers.
- Post your values everywhere, and ask your employees and visitors to hold you and your company to them. Without visibility and support, core values are meaningless.

14

Establish a Company Vision and Get Out of the Way

One of the best tools I was ever taught was how to project my life and our company into the future. Mastering this has had dramatic effects on my personal life, as well as our business.

When I was a member of Vistage, I heard a presentation given by Dr. Tom Hill. He was a mature guy with white hair and a beard, but he had the vim and vigor of a much younger man. He looked like he'd discovered the fountain of youth. Dr. Hill said that he was a disciple of Jim Rohn, a personal development guru. Dr. Hill combined Jim Rohn's teachings with several others he'd come across in his pursuit of personal development to create a course he named Designing the Exceptional Life.

I took Dr. Hill's yearlong, online course, which helped me achieve greater balance in my life and learn how to dream and achieve bigger. The course had several components. One was to identify if you were left-brained or right-brained and to learn how to identify those traits in others so you could better communicate with them.

I plotted where I thought I was on a scale from one to ten in six areas of life: spiritual, health, relationships, emotional, intellectual, and financial. There was a ton of value created when I wrote down what my perfect life would look like in six years. I wrote in present tense, as if I was already there, and I included all six areas. I even included the smells and sounds to trick my brain into thinking that it had already happened. That vision became my reality. The secret was to write my six-year perfect world around SMART goals (Specific, Measurable, Achievable, Realistic, and Timely).

Then I had to reverse-engineer my goals into my three-year SMART goals, my eighteen-month SMART goals, all the way down to what I'd do in the next ninety days. I defined what areas needed work and what measures I'd take to succeed.

Dr. Hill also prescribed several practices to follow. One practice was to get away from the outside world and your friends and family for a three-day "solitude retreat" at least once a year. It's a time to be silent and reflect on your life, to journal about the people and things you are grateful for, and to identify areas where you need to improve in order to become the best version of you.

This whole notion of creating a reality from my dreams and vision was really appealing. This is how our futures get changed: someone dares to dream of an improvement in the future and does everything to focus on that dream to make it a reality. Suddenly, it becomes a reality that affects the lives of millions of people. (Think Steve Jobs and the iPhone.)

I followed these practices and, after I experienced some successes, I shared the process with our directors in a strategic planning meeting. Much to my surprise, the director who'd achieved the most financial success and was the most experienced career-wise spoke out first and declared that he needed more balance in his life!

His response made me want to take this idea to the next level. So before we had our next meeting with all the senior managers, I wrote, "Our perfect company in six years." That was in September 2008. In that missive, I wrote in present tense about where we'd be in size, in financials, and in leadership in September 2014.

Vision: Our perfect company in six years

"It's late September 2014, and the air is still hot in Phoenix, much like the performance of our company these past six years! I'm now sixty years old, and life has been very kind to me. I have a wonderful wife and kids and a gaggle of grandchildren. Our business growth has been amazing. I'm now the chairman and completely out of the day-to-day operations, but I split my time between traveling to our scattered locations to ensure that our culture is thriving and keeping up with our volunteer projects in the communities we serve.

I'm privileged to work with some of the best people in our industry. We have a new CEO who replaced me, and several new division presidents. We recently sold one of our five business units to reinvest and focus on our other four lines. These four units are thriving, with total gross revenues in nine figures.

We made huge investments in capital and people to get where we are today. We have the attitude and conviction that we're the right choice for any contract, and we've been exceptionable at convincing our customers and partners of the same.

Our cab companies are doing over $50 million per year in gross lease sales. We're the number-one choice with our public and private clients. Our call center dispatches an average of over twelve thousand trips per day, and it runs like a clock. Our shops maintain over one thousand taxicabs, and they're always the cleanest and best maintained in our markets. Our claims record is the envy of the industry and almost gives us an unfair advantage when we compete on price.

Our transit division manages at least three transit centers and two Dial-a-Ride programs and has revenues approaching $100 million. We have parlayed the over thirty-year experience of our organization and the untold experience of our seasoned staff to reach the point that we are considered a model operator by the industry. We are now poised to grow to $1 billion by 2020.

Our transportation management company has taken on a life of its own. It is first on anyone's list to call to solve any transportation problem. No job is too big or too small for this group. It utilizes not only both its related companies' assets, but also outside partners that help achieve our goals.

We have two other divisions: one that we built and decided to sell and another that's only three years old but has a bright future with many opportunities for our employees. I'm so proud of our organization. We are a cohesive group of people who really like each other and take great pride in our work—not only for the money and satisfaction of a job well done, but also to make our communities better places to live.

Speaking of money, our company has created five millionaires and hopes to create five times that number over the next six years. Every one of our offices has the "Total Transit touch" that makes it a great place to spend our workdays.

Yes, the weather is still warm, but we see every day as a perfect day to achieve our vision."

I wrote that in September 2008 without really knowing how we would achieve those goals, but with every intention of achieving them. When I presented this to our managers, they could envision where they fit into this vision of the future—and it was a place they wanted to go. Their excitement was off the charts. The numbers I proposed were staggering compared to our size in 2008; no other cab company in the country was achieving anything near those numbers.

This exercise led us to refine our company vision and change it to this:

> **The vision of Total Transit is to be a revolutionary organization responsible for transporting more passengers than any other company in America.**

Now that was a bold statement. Everyone knew that if we wanted to achieve it, we'd have to have huge growth and make major changes to our organization. We made a point to state that we'd be revolutionary. We couldn't achieve this vision without being disruptive. We would blaze a new trail.

We knew we couldn't achieve that vision without national expansion, although when we wrote it, we didn't know what structure would get us there. But having defined the goal, our task was to figure out a way to make it happen.

I followed up that session with an offer to hold personal coaching classes every week for a year, in nine areas of life—Dr. Hill's six areas, plus career, community, and recreation. Everyone who participated had to envision his or her perfect life in six years, as well as a perfect career, even if that meant the individual was no longer in our employ.

We had around twenty-five students, and I created a curriculum based on Dr. Hill's that reflected my own spin and a few additional resources. One of those resources was Dave Ramsey's Financial Peace University, which I became certified to teach to our employees. We eventually touched over 150 employees with that program and changed the trajectory of many employees' lives and that of their families.

What made me feel really great was when they pulled me aside or sent a note to tell me about their success and what it meant to them and their families. How could you ask for more?

One of our mechanics, Chuck, came to the Financial Peace class with his wife. They were renting a house, had no savings, and owed thousands for mechanic's school and to the tool man; and, of course, they also had credit card debt. Within two years Chuck had paid off all that debt. They bought a repossessed house for less than its real value and had instant equity. Chuck became more financially successful than anyone in his family, including his parents and grandparents. Chuck and his wife had learned how to break the chains of debt that hold so many back.

We continue to rewrite our six-year vision every eighteen months (eighteen months is the amount of time it takes to get through each growth curve), and we change anything that needs to be changed to reflect the current environment.

Maybe you're saying, "That sounds great, but I don't have the time to do that in my company."

I didn't have the time either, and the fact is that we wouldn't be so far along if I hadn't let go of all my duties so I could concentrate on the big picture. This was my way to add value to the organization.

So what did things look like in September 2014? Incredibly, *we didn't dream big enough*. We blew way past almost every target we set in September 2008! That just proves what you can achieve when everyone on the team works hard toward a shared vision. We were all in the same boat, and we all rowed in unison.

So what about reaching $1 billion in sales that we put out there in 2008 as our goal for 2020? We have every intention to hit and exceed that number as well. We developed what we call the 10x growth strategy, meaning that we grow our organization tenfold every six years. We did some quick math to figure out how to get there and found that we have to grow an average of almost 50 percent per year. Fifty percent growth is within reach if you have a large enough marketplace and a superior offering, and we knew we couldn't achieve this by operating only in the Arizona market.

It's really astounding what you can accomplish in twelve years, or two six-year growth cycles. Years one through six can see a $10 million company turn into a $100 million operation. That's very impressive; however, if years seven through twelve see that same growth, your $100 million company becomes a $1 billion operation. It's mind-blowing to think that a little $10 million company could become a $1 billion behemoth in just twelve years. Mind-blowing, but possible.

When you and your team see the possibility of accomplishing this growth, you'll look at your business totally differently. I remember when we hit $50 million in annual sales and looked six years out and saw the path to $500 million. The company mindset magically changes, and you no longer operate like a $50 million operation, because you'll soon be a $500 million entity. So you think of your company as a $500 million operation that just doesn't have the sales yet. The task is to obtain that growth, which practically becomes a self-fulfilling mindset.

Creating a vision is one way we created a better business, but that's only part of the secret. There also were some things I had to do on a personal level to crack the code and move the company to the next level.

Lessons Learned

- Writing a believable, achievable present-tense vision for your company and getting buy-in from your leaders and employees is your most powerful tool as a business owner.
- Helping your employees deal with their personal challenges makes the whole team stronger.

15

Want a Better Business? Become a Better Person.

A business is a reflection of its owner. If the owner isn't a good person, the business will reflect that weakness. Likewise, a principled owner's actions will be reflected throughout the organization.

I've seen it from both sides. A few years ago, I was in a filthy store where the service and selection were terrible. I walked out without buying anything, and I couldn't help but wonder what kind of sad SOB owned that place. Could the owner really be proud to own it, and did he or she think anyone would become a repeat customer?

I had the same experience with our business. In the early years, we wanted to rent a property for a new satellite office.

The property manager said, "I've seen your old cars. I wouldn't ride in one, and I don't want them leaking oil on my parking lot."

Ouch! A comment like that really stings, but there was truth to it. If you have any pride at all, you'll see it in another light and use the new insight to drive improvements in your operation.

I started to spot-check our cabs in the parking lot, and if I didn't feel like a vehicle was nice enough to put my mother in, we pulled it off the fleet to refurbish or retire it. This hurt in the early days because money was tight, but we started to develop a reputation for the nicest cabs on the street.

In the later years, people said things like, "You own that business? Wow! I see your cars everywhere, and they look great. You must really feel proud."

Or I drive down the road and see our vehicles at almost every corner. They all look sharp and have conscientious, safe drivers behind the wheel. And I think to myself, *If I weren't already the owner of that business, I'd want to be!*

If your business is a reflection of who you are, then you need to be the best possible version of yourself. It's just not possible to separate the two.

When you become the best version of you, you can give your best to everyone, including your family and business associates. It makes you a better family member and a better businessperson because you refuse to settle for what's average or just good. Remember what I said earlier: being good is the greatest enemy of becoming great.

Your business will outgrow the abilities of many of its employees, and it will outgrow you, too, if you don't watch out. Your abilities must grow as your business gets more and more complex.

Most of us don't naturally operate at our highest level. To do so takes discipline and a lot of hard work. So let's talk about some of the tools, and there are many in self-improvement, to get you there.

One of the first things is to get a good coach, mentor, or teacher to lead you through the process. But even the best teacher in the world won't do you any good unless you follow their lead and are ready to grow.

It's also difficult to figure out who will be the right mentor. I contracted with Dr. Tom Hill. He'd already become a financial success when he asked himself, "What next? Where do I go now?" He wrote the book *Living at the Summit* to address the "what next" question and decided to give back by teaching others the lessons he'd learned.

I think this is the best kind of teacher. I see so many life coaches who haven't really done anything, but they feel qualified to give advice and charge for it. I'd rather sit at the knee of someone who's made himself into someone I admire. I want to hear what worked for them, not a theory about what works.

I'd like to share the highlights of what I learned and how these insights and tools helped both our business and me. The rest of this chapter may seem a little "out there," but it's from some of that "woo-woo" that our secret sauce reveals itself.

What's the path to becoming the best version of yourself? Some of this was very easy and natural for me, but I struggled with other parts. Besides the coaching and the training, you'll need to read and learn from an assortment of self-improvement books. Like most important life lessons, you can't just sit in class or attend a lecture. You have to immerse yourself in the process to get the results you want. Your business is growing, so you'd better be growing as well if you want to be relevant.

In the last chapter, I stressed how important it is to create a vision for your perfect future and to write it out in the present tense. That is just the start. To achieve real growth, you have to seek it out on your own path. You have to have an appetite for growth and change, and you'll find it as your curiosity leads you from one idea to the next. Not everything you read will hit home. Just keep seeking, and you'll find the journey is so worth it.

I also mentioned that we held classes for our managers and supervisors for a full year to help them down this path. I warned them up front that having me as a teacher was a lot like having a sixth grader teach the fourth grade. I'd just completed the lessons online with Dr. Hill myself, and I promised to try my best.

Truth is, I never planned to go down this path. I'm a pretty private person, and all this sharing isn't really in my nature. But when one of my senior managers said he wanted to be more balanced, it made me leave my comfort zone for the good of our people and our organization. Anything worth doing is worth doing well, and I was going to give it my best shot.

I rewrote many of the lessons, and it took several hours each week to prepare for class, do the research, and write the lessons. I also gave out assignments, and I met with the participants to discuss their progress if they wanted. I had time to do this because I'd turned the day-to-day operations of the business over to others.

Preparing a class on spirituality required research on mysticism, meditation, as well as traditional and nontraditional faiths. We had Buddhist and Chi healers speak, and everyone seemed to gain a lot from the exploration. I was worried that discussing spirituality and relationships would be taboo at work, but everyone wanted to improve their lives.

I highly recommend this kind of interaction with your team because we all got a chance to understand each other better. I think I got more out of the lessons than any of our employees.

That year made me a better person. I meditated for an hour a day following the Holosync® program, and it helped transform me to a better version of myself. All of the research led me to read more books over a few years than I'd read in my entire life. I read one nonfiction or self-help book after another and ended up buying and reading hundreds of books. This reintroduced me to my love of reading, which I'd forgotten.

Around that same time, I also took lessons and read books about how to form a Mastermind group. A Mastermind group is a small number of people who meet on a regular basis to discuss a common theme.

We formed our Mastermind group around the theme of rapid growth for our organizations, specifically, how to increase our size tenfold in six years. To accomplish this, you have to grow an average of just under fifty percent a year, so our growth rate of forty to forty-five percent was no fluke. We had about ten entrepreneurs from around the country who all wanted to grow their companies to the next level.

The funny thing is that when I worked on someone else's problem, the solution to one of my own often revealed itself. We would hold each other accountable and report our progress.

After about eighteen months, the Mastermind group played itself out. We had formed a tight bond, but we met online every week and in person once a quarter, and it took its toll. Several members made phenomenal progress, and others struggled. But it felt like some members and their businesses were set free, mine included.

The bottom line is that I had to be a bigger, more well-read, and more well-rounded person to support the weight of a business that looked nothing like the business we'd started with. It's not just your people, processes, and facilities that have to improve to support your growth to an enterprise-size business. You must make the leap as well.

Lessons Learned

- Your business is a reflection of the owner. You can't overlook its flaws. You have to maintain your standards.
- Just like your business can outgrow your leaders, it can outgrow the owner. You have to become the best version of yourself to keep up.
- There's no downside to becoming a better person.

16

Go into Overdrive to Head Off Disruption

Your business is working for you now, and you have the freedom and income you wanted. Now what? You built a successful business, and you have a comfortable lifestyle—why not quit right there? What's wrong with building up a nice business that affords you a great lifestyle? In the past, that might have worked; but in this age of disruption, it often won't.

Even before Amazon arrived and disrupted the retail business, I'd see a new category of merchandise at Costco for a price a local retailer couldn't even buy it for as a dealer. And I'd say to myself, *I'm sure glad we don't sell that because no one would pay our price if they could get it at Costco for less.*

Many years ago, we bought a car stereo from Costco to put in one of our kids' car. We took it to a car stereo shop to have the installer put it in.

The owner came out and said, "We sell that same unit. Where did you buy it, and can I ask you how much you paid?"

Then he looked up the stereo and speakers in his book and said, "You paid less than what I can get it for as a dealer!" I could see the look of gloom in his eyes. He knew his business was in trouble.

This is why it's so important that once your primary business is at a certain scale and profitability, you must diversify, innovate, and expand. When your business reaches the point where it throws off enough money to keep you comfortable and is on firm footing, it's important to find a way to invest the excess to achieve those goals. Our story is a warning.

One of our first goals was to create one of the top cab companies in the nation. We did exactly that, and we were the envy of our industry. The cab company made millions of dollars a year, far more than we needed personally.

We'd always plowed money back into the business, but we could see a future where the cab business was no longer our main business and, in fact, was a smaller piece of the overall organization. So we took our excess revenues and instead of investing the money in our core operation, we looked for other complementary areas where we could invest.

We invested in things that no one who wanted to just operate a local cab company would invest in. We moved everything we could to the cloud, so we could operate seamlessly across our platforms in any jurisdiction. We devised ways to disrupt businesses where we already operated or wanted to operate, such as public transit and medical transportation management.

I wish we could say that we saw the disruption to the taxi business years before it happened, but we didn't. You never know what a "black swan event" will look like in your industry, or when it will come. A black swan is an event or occurrence that deviates from what is normally expected and is extremely difficult to predict. You just have to do everything in your power as an owner and a leader to protect your business.

We got a chance to disrupt the Dial-a-Ride business in public transportation with our virtual platform, and we saw that we were pretty good at taking care of large medical accounts. So we morphed that business into a transportation management division that would allow us to grow nationally. We didn't have a true disruptive, or differentiated, model at first, but we always gave our best effort to exceed the customer's expectations.

Then, along came Uber, and a total disruption hit the cab business. (For more about how Uber affected our company, see chapter 18.) Suddenly, owning the largest or best cab company in the country was like owning the best buggy whip company after the Model T. It became almost irrelevant, except for the way we responded.

We felt that the personal cash cab business was at great risk, so we needed to make our service even better. That's one of the reasons we bought a technology company. We also put more focus on our account business and kept it growing. We were tasked to grow by 40 percent or more a year, and we couldn't do that without a complete overhaul of our business model. Failure wasn't an option. We had a 10x growth strategy, and we had to stay the course. This is what allowed us to not only survive the disruption to our industry, but also to thrive and disrupt another industry as well.

If we had continued to operate the business as usual, we would have had more money in the short term, but we might have gone out of business in the long run.

This is why I stress that you must always keep some part, or maybe even your whole organization, in the innovation and expansion stage. You must expand your existing businesses into new markets and look for ideas and industries that complement your businesses to diversify your offerings and protect your organization from the inevitable disruptions that no one can foresee.

Lessons Learned

- Disruption will touch almost every business segment into the foreseeable future.
- You never know when a black swan event will hit your business or what it will look like.
- Once your main line is established, start expanding and innovating.

17

Blaze Your Own Bold Path

If your company does what everyone else does, are you adding value? Have you reexamined your industry and markets to see if change is needed? Do you consistently experiment with new ideas on a smaller scale to see if an idea has merit? And if it does, do you jump in with both feet?

You don't have to invent all these improvements. You might see a slick payment system that can enhance the customer experience in a completely different industry. Can you adopt that technology, or something similar, in your business to deliver that same satisfaction to your customers?

Times are changing for all businesses. The rules that used to apply are changing at a rapid pace, and you and your company have to be part of that change. Hopefully, you're on the leading edge to bring value and relevancy to your company.

The cab business is a dirty business. We have vehicles on the road twenty-four hours a day with drivers in them for twelve-hour shifts. The standard vehicle for most cab companies in the US was a former police car, either a Chevy Caprice or a Ford Crown Victoria.

In 2007, our fleet was composed mostly of late-model Crown Victorias.

We bought only the latest models at auction. Then we brought them into the shop to give them a makeover with all new paint and upholstery, and we went over any mechanical issues from front to back. Our cabs looked so good that when they hit the line, one new general manager thought we'd bought them all new. But even though they looked nice, they were gas-guzzlers and polluters.

Our daughter, Danielle, was attending the University of San Francisco at the time, and she'd become quite the tree-hugger. She liked to tell me that we could improve our environmental impact if we converted to hybrids.

"Dad," she said, "you need to clean up your act. There's a more responsible way to put a fleet on the road."

I took her comments to heart because I felt guilty about the environmental impact that comes from running a large fleet. But any solution we attempted had to make financial sense as well.

We started to buy and test different hybrids, but we weren't sold on any of them. The Honda Civic hybrid had a rough transition between modes, and the Ford Escape hybrids didn't deliver the gas savings necessary to make them relevant. My own preconceived notion was that the Prius was too small and frail to be a taxi. I called a Toyota dealer, and the salesman said he'd bring one by so we could see it up close.

I told him my concerns, and he said, "You've never sat in the back seat have you?"

"No," I admitted. "They just seem like they would be too small."

He brought a Prius over, and two other big guys and I climbed in the back seat. I couldn't get over how much room we had. Not only were we not cramped on hip space, our knees didn't hit the back of the front seat. I was truly astounded, and we put in an order for twenty of them that day.

We still weren't convinced that the Prius would hold up to the twenty-four-hour double shifts that taxis are subjected to, so we visited a Canadian cab company in Vancouver, British Columbia, that had run them for a couple of years. They confirmed that they'd had a great experience with them.

This might be a good place to explain how most cab companies operate. Cab companies are basically leasing companies. The drivers don't pay just for the use of our vehicles; they also pay for access to our calls. Some cities are tightly regulated, and people drive the existing fleets' cabs because the companies have the legal permits necessary to operate in their jurisdiction. This gives the permit–or medallion holders–a bit of a monopoly, and it's mostly left up to the drivers to develop their own business.

We operate a little differently in Arizona because we have a deregulated open-entry system. So the way we added value was by making sure our drivers had enough work. Our business development efforts, the quality control of both our vehicles and our drivers, and the steps we took to ensure we were easy to do business with paid their dividends, and we created the busiest taxi dispatch company in the nation.

That allowed us to charge higher rates to our drivers, who still made more money than they could with the competition. Once the Prius entered our fleet, the drivers took home more money through lower fuel expense; and, once they got used to the fuel savings, they didn't want to drive a Crown Vic.

We decided to release the Priuses into our fleet on Earth Day, April 22, 2008. We did a PR blitz that we called the Prius Project, and because each Prius promised to save us four thousand gallons of fuel per year, we upped our commitment and bought 250 vehicles, for a projected annual fuel savings of one million gallons. No company in North America operated Prius cabs at that scale.

At this time, a lot of companies said that they were "green," but many were actually "green washing." They didn't really live up to their claims; they just wanted the positive PR. We got a ton of press coverage that Earth Day, but there was one news report that stood out. It was put together by a young reporter from a local television station who wanted to expose the green-washing practice. She came in with cameras rolling and said, "Okay, show me your hybrid." She was shocked when we showed her twenty fully converted, bright green Discount Cab Prius taxis.

I tell this story because you don't know where your best ideas will come from—in this case, my daughter—or where a change will lead your company. The cost to transform our fleet was significant; we went from $5,000 Crown Victorias to $22,000 Prius cabs. Eventually, we had over 900 Prius cabs, which represented a hefty investment of over $20 million but gave us impressive annual savings of over three million gallons of fuel.

Still, that's a huge investment. How did we pay for it? The drivers saved about $40 per day in fuel, and we charged them $20 a day more for the Prius. This made our car payment for us, and each driver netted $20 a day more and got to drive a nicer, newer car.

Our maintenance on the Crown Victoria ran about twelve cents per mile; the Prius, over its life, ran five cents per mile. This represented an additional savings of $28,000 over the 400,000-mile life of the vehicle. These savings greatly increased our net revenues.

The biggest surprise was how our drivers, the riders, and the public reacted. Our fleet stood out from the rest and elevated the public opinion of our company to new heights. They could clearly see we weren't like the rest, and our bright lime-green modern hybrid vehicles were everywhere. We kicked the Prius movement off with the campaign, "Green Cabs for Blue Skies." We later switched to, "We Drive People Happy." Both campaigns drove our business skyward.

Our dispatched trips increased to an average of 15,000 per day, making our dispatch center the busiest in the US. Our Prius fleet was the largest in North America, and we started winning a litany of awards. These awards included Arizona (AZ) Most Admired CEO; AZ Top 25 Fastest-Growing Companies and 50 largest many times; AZ Green Pioneer award; EY Entrepreneur of the Year finalist; Best Places to Work; Healthiest Employer; Innovative Company of the Year; and The Innovation in Entrepreneurship Award from Arizona State University's W. P. Carey School of Business. And my alma mater, the University of Arkansas Sam Walton College of Business, named me the Alumni Entrepreneur of the Year in 2013.

The awards were almost an embarrassment. We didn't invent the Prius, and we weren't even the first cab company to operate them. We just adopted them into our business model at an unprecedented scale.

Today, you see them in fleets everywhere, and we like to think our success had something to do with that.

We even were visited by Toyota engineers from Japan who wanted to learn about the methods our shop technicians had developed to prolong the battery life. Toyota actually purchased one of our high-mileage cabs and shipped it to Japan so their engineers could disassemble it and check the condition of all the components, as part of their continuing improvement process.

We took another chance on a different innovation and decided to take a risk when we received a Request for Proposal from the local transit agency for a small Dial-a-Ride project in Northwest Phoenix. We submitted a proposal to operate a traditional DAR as requested in the RFP. The transit agency invited us in to explain how we'd perform the service.

I described how we could do what they requested and how much it would cost. Then I stopped and said, "But if it was my money, that's not how I'd do it, and as a taxpayer I feel like it is my money."

The room got quiet, and I proceeded to explain what we called the Virtual DAR model.

A traditional model uses employee drivers, a limited fleet, and separate offices and shops. I described how we could do this in-house and use our existing call center and shop, and train our drivers to the same standards that the transit authority required. When we got a DAR call, the taxi driver would operate as a DAR driver; when the trip was over, he'd go back to operating as a regular cab driver. This way, we'd charge only for the services that were needed. Instead of having the constraints of a fixed fleet size, we were flexible enough to commit from five to five hundred cars to their service at any given time.

The transit agency thanked us for our time and sent us on our way. I called Mike Pinckard, who was attending Harvard at that time, and with a grimace told him, "I probably blew a good deal, but I had to let them know how I felt."

We didn't hear back from them for several weeks, which usually isn't a good sign. They finally reached out and said they wanted to meet us in our boardroom. They didn't tell us anything more. At the meeting, their CEO opened the discussion by saying, "We heard what you said, and we agree with you. However, it's such a departure from what we asked for that we have to issue a new RFP."

Well, we bid on the RFP and won it! The service proved to be a huge hit with the DAR riders, we saved the municipalities over 35 percent, and the service was leagues better than what they would have gotten. This win set us up for a huge DAR contract in the East Valley, which was written so that our model fit the need. We bid and were successful on a contract that had formerly cost the municipalities and their taxpayers $10 million a year. Our bid was $6.5 million, and our service was miles better than what they had before. Because our model is so flexible and efficient, we still made a decent profit, and it resulted in significant new business for our cab drivers.

Mike, our CEO, initiated another leap. He wanted to innovate our leasing arrangement with our contract drivers and suggested we change the way we charged our drivers for their leases, to better reflect their use of company services. We charged a flat lease that varied by the day of the week, by the shift (day or night shift), and by vehicle type. He suggested that we charge a small fixed lease and a variable lease that reflected the amount of services the drivers actually consumed. That way, a driver who got all his work off our system would pay more for his lease, and a contractor who developed his own business would pay less.

The drivers certainly weren't sold at first. They saw the new plan as a way for us to get more money out of them. The opposite is actually what our numbers showed. Why would we devise a formula that would pay us less? As the drivers adapted to this system, they encouraged their good fares to call them directly for a more personalized service. This took the weight of these calls off the call center, and we saw our call center costs go down. We also saw more cars going out with fewer calls per shift necessary for their success. This idea resulted, much like our Prius Project, in a win-win-win for our customers, our drivers, and our company.

I'm not saying that all of our ideas were this successful. They certainly weren't. But the process of constantly railing against the status quo is the very mindset that helped us confront the biggest challenge and disruption to our industry. Everything we'd done up to this point was now at risk.

Lessons Learned

- If you offer the same thing everyone else does, you're not adding value to the marketplace.
- Do you see a great innovation in another industry or market that you think will work in yours? Give it your best shot.
- When your business is going great is when you should look for ways to improve your offerings, not when you're forced to.

18

Taking On the Uber Challenge

Disruptive innovation is knocking on the door of every business. Artificial intelligence and new ways to communicate will continue to disrupt every industry for the foreseeable future. Your only option is to figure out how to handle it when it hits yours.

The taxicab business was pretty much unchanged for one hundred years, and that became the problem. Most states and municipalities regulate taxis to a high degree. The supply of vehicles is restricted, which allowed municipalities to sell licenses to operate taxis, called medallions, for a short-term windfall for the municipality. That medallion protects the owner from competition.

This regulation produced a myriad of problems. A secondary market drove medallion prices in markets like New York City to over $1million each, which is what drove fares higher. The drivers had to take in more money to cover their vehicle leases as well as the medallion fee, so the meter rate had to be higher to cover this cost.

The restriction of medallions in most markets created a "race to the bottom" for taxi service. It made no sense for a fleet owner to put out anything more than a barely acceptable product because doing otherwise would increase demand for more cabs than they had licenses to fulfill. It didn't matter if a company with one hundred permits had business for one hundred cabs per hour or five hundred cabs per hour because there was no way for them to service any excess demand. Thus, cab companies across the country got a richly deserved terrible reputation.

They not only didn't know how to compete, they didn't have to compete. They could make a good living just by keeping their cabs full and their expenses down.

The cab companies never knew what hit them when the transportation network companies (TNCs) such as Uber and Lyft entered their marketplaces. They had always been protected and didn't know how to compete, and this disruption quickly started to kill their leasing operations.

Remember our five stages of business development? These companies were in the mature stage. They hadn't reinvested in their product, which made them especially vulnerable to this new competition. They not only faced decline but their demise.

Many of them turned to their regulators to protect them, and they tried to make the TNCs adhere to the same rules that they had to follow. The problem was that the TNCs were well funded, and they knew how to compete. They rallied their riders and drivers behind their cause. The public loved the TNCs and mostly hated their local cab service.

We were highly aware of the actions being taken by the TNCs, and we could see their disruptive nature would change our world forever, in both positive and negative ways. They created a better mousetrap with ease of use, a flexible fleet to meet demand, and the destruction of the regulations that had protected the taxi industry in most markets for years.

Fortunately, we had a different operation than most other cab companies. Arizona is the largest deregulated market in the United States. We had no protection granted by medallions or regulators and none of their restrictions. We had no guarantee of vehicles on the street. Instead, we had to compete every day. We had to offer the best service and be as easy to work with as possible, which is how we grew from two Discount Cab vehicles to almost twelve hundred after thirty years in business. That is why we have the busiest taxi call center in the United States in a place that isn't considered a taxi town like New York, Chicago, or San Francisco.

When we attended the first taxicab convention after Uber started, it was all anyone could talk about. Uber initially offered Lincoln Town Cars at a taxi price. All over the country, people who hated their stinky, unreliable cab service embraced this new way to ride.

We thought that the cab companies deserved to lose much of this formerly protected business. The low threshold of service and quality came back to bite many underperforming operators. I remember one large operator said he'd already lost 30 percent of his business. He asked how we were doing after Uber, and we told him that our calls were actually up. We offered reliable service at a good price and had developed a pretty loyal customer base.

It wasn't until a couple of years later that Uber adopted Lyft's shared economy platform. With this service, the drivers use their own privately insured vehicles instead of leasing a commercial vehicle with commercial insurance. They operate at rates we couldn't get near with our fully insured, commercial platform.

It was very controversial at the time because that model was put in place before adequate insurance was secured. These heavily backed players figured they could self-insure their way through that issue, and an insurance solution would be forthcoming. They were right. They could also flex the size of their fleet on the street to meet demand, because it was a virtual fleet. We knew we were going to have to change to compete.

This was never more apparent than when we found out that several of our call center personnel had ordered these low-priced, shared-ride vehicles instead of taking our employee-discounted cabs to get to work. It wasn't too long after the TNCs entered our marketplace that we started to see a year-over-year decline in cash cab rides. Luckily, we were still growing our commercial account sales at a record pace, which helped soften the blow, but we knew it wouldn't be enough to take us into the future.

We had an appetite for change and constantly looked for ways to improve our product, even if it meant we had to turn our back on some traditions and processes that got us where we were. Our CEO came back from an industry meeting and said he thought we should either buy a technology company or start one. I'd thought for some time that the traditional dispatch vendors weren't meeting our needs and agreed we should pursue that idea. But we had no idea how we could afford to buy a technology company, and we sure didn't have any experience running one. If we made this decision, we were afraid it would be a distraction from our primary business of running a transportation company.

The solution came to us after we met with the owners of a small technology operation in San Diego with whom we had a relationship. We were the largest user of their text-based taxi-ordering service, and they had developed a simple app but lacked the funding to develop it further. At first, it was just two guys and some outsourced programmers.

The CEO of this company, Josh Komenda, had a full-time job with a large technology company. We got him to sell his company to us, quit his job, and work full time on this new project. We wanted this business to grow outside our influence and with minimal distractions to our transportation companies, so we kept it in San Diego. The technology company was rebranded 2PointB and continued to develop and grow until we produced a product that could compete with the TNCs. Or so we thought.

We developed a consumer-facing app as well as a driver app. We started operating in Arizona and offered the solution to other taxi operators around the country, but they were very skeptical. We soon found we couldn't compete with the incentives that the well-funded TNCs offered their customers to ride in their cars. Their cost of customer acquisition is tremendous.

When I had to travel in other parts of the country, Lyft gave me so many credits to take their rides that they were practically free. We thought if we mined our existing customer base, and that of other traditional operators, it would solve the expensive acquisition of customers that the new TNCs faced.

The problem was that our taxi model still had too much overhead to allow us to compete unless we provided a TNC option, which we were willing to do.

But other operators shunned the idea. Also, the TNCs were so well funded that they could operate at a huge loss, and at unsustainable rates, by paying their drivers more than they charged the customer.

It isn't unusual for these startups to do $1 billion in ride revenue and lose an additional $1 billion. For every dollar they took in, they spent two. We couldn't afford to go this route because we were internally funded. This helped us decide that we had to refocus our efforts.

We chose to focus on the positives in this model and looked at what other divisions could benefit from this technology. We'd been expanding our transportation management division, and we could see that nonemergency medical transportation would be harder for the TNCs to pierce.

Eventually, we created a whole new company with a disruptive solution for healthcare logistics. We went from being the disrupted in our cab business to the disrupter in the multibillion-dollar transportation management industry.

We named our new company Veyo. This company has a similar advantage over the existing brokers and providers of medical transportation that the TNCs had over the cab companies. The large transportation management companies went from not knowing who we were to finding that they were losing large accounts to us and couldn't compete against our model.

We conceived an entire supply-chain solution that gives our customers, and us, real-time transparency into their patient transportation. After three years of development, our solution is light years ahead of our competition.

We also utilize our own fleet of TNC vehicles to provide better, more effective transportation services to our customers. We fully vetted the idea with our existing transportation management customers. We even fed seven thousand calls a day from our taxi fleet into Veyo's new virtual fleet.

We sacrificed one business for the other to get the kind of volume we needed to prove our concept. We're being awarded new business all over the country and can go into underserved markets and immediately ramp up supply of this virtual fleet to meet our customers' needs.

Other former leaders in the taxi business find their companies are on the outs with the riding public, and they're faced with a severe decline in revenue. They have few options. This is why I emphasize that you must not only be on the constant lookout for change in your industry, but you also must spend the time and effort necessary to change your model or use technology to disrupt whatever market you serve. If you don't, I guarantee you that someone else will, and it could wipe out all you've created in the past, overnight.

Lessons Learned

- Is your industry being disrupted? Think about how you can be the disrupter, not the victim.

19

What's Life Like After This Transition?

So, was all the hard work worth it? How is life different today for our family, our employees, our leaders, and me?

I'm not going to lie. Life is pretty damn good. Let me tell you about last week.

Last week, we had so many balls in the air. We received unsolicited offers to purchase one of our divisions from several different buyers. We were also waiting to hear if we'd been awarded two major contracts we bid on. We had a service issue in one area of the country that needed immediate attention. We had meetings with investment bankers and mergers and acquisition people from both companies on both coasts.

These meetings and issues are critical to our future and have to be handled correctly. We have numbers to hit and a reputation of service we have to protect.

What did I do all week? I attended a birthday party and a wedding in Mexico where I had no cell service. I did have sketchy Wi-Fi that allowed me to check email and messages, but we would have been fine with nothing.

We had a great time with a couple of our kids and grandchildren and some pleasant time offline. My three-year-old and five-year-old grandsons, whose dad is from Mexico, speak way better Spanish than me, and it was fun using them as interpreters.

The entire time we were gone, no one from the office tried to contact me. Our team is truly empowered to make all the necessary decisions. They are graded and rewarded by metrics, and their actions are bound to our core principles. No one has to wait to hear what I think before they act.

Of course, I'm still interested in what's going on and how we're performing. I'm just no longer a slave to the business. Mike and his team handled the M&A guys and moved that process along. We were awarded both contracts. One was for over $50 million annually and was the largest single contract in our company's history! A team jumped on the service issue and has a plan to resolve it.

I knew nothing about what progress was made until I came in on Monday and sat down with Mike. I knew we had a lot going on, but I have so much confidence in our team that I wasn't worried. Mike went through the meetings and outcomes, and gave me a status report on where we were and what we had coming up. After our briefing, which covered as much personal business as company business, I was free to pursue whatever agenda I wanted to pursue.

This week, I'll get this book finished. Next week, who knows? It will be whatever I want it to be. That's what it's like for me to live "my perfect life," and it can be that way for you as well.

About the Author

A multitalented businessman, Craig Hughes loves everything about business. He is the founder and chairman of Total Transit, Inc., and he learned the ropes through trial and error. During this journey he found his own way to business success.

Although he was once the obstacle to his company's growth, Craig figured out how to let go of the day-to-day duties that were holding his company back so he could focus on the vision. With the support of his wife, Chris, and the leadership of his CEO, Mike Pinckard, he created a unique company with amazing growth and profitability from a small, unassuming taxi business.

Craig and Chris live in Scottsdale, Arizona, and are delighted that all of their children and grandchildren live in Arizona, too. They formed a charitable foundation in 2009 and continue to work to improve the communities they serve.

Made in the USA
Middletown, DE
14 December 2019